Keyboarding for Business

Susan Burke and Maureen Reynolds

Gill & Macmillan

Published in Ireland by
Gill & Macmillan Ltd
Goldenbridge Dublin 8
with associated companies throughout the world

© Susan Burke and Maureen Reynolds 1993

0 7171 2090 2

Designed by The Unlimited Design Company, Dublin

Print origination in Ireland by
Seton Music Graphics Ltd, Bantry, Co. Cork

Printed in Ireland by
ColourBooks Ltd, Dublin

www.gillmacmillan.ie

Contents

Preface

With the increased availability of computer technology, the skill of keyboarding has become a vital one for success in business. This book caters for business students who wish to acquire the basic skills of keyboarding and to gain familiarity with the variety of documents they are likely to encounter. All of the exercises can be keyed on either a typewriter or computer keyboard.

The authors have many years teaching experience of both Typewriting and Information Technology in addition to practical work experience. The knowledge they have gained is reflected in the modern style of display used throughout the book.

Acknowledgements

The authors would like to thank the following: An Bord Tráchtála, Bord Iascaigh Mhara, the Environmental Information Service and Commodore Computers for giving permission to reproduce text. Thanks also to Carmen Tarifa, Karen Breuer, Annick Ferre and Sophie Valette for checking foreign language text.

In particular we would like to acknowledge our colleague, Margot Fee, who painstakingly proof-read the text and whose observations were very much appreciated.

The Commodore SSL386sx-20

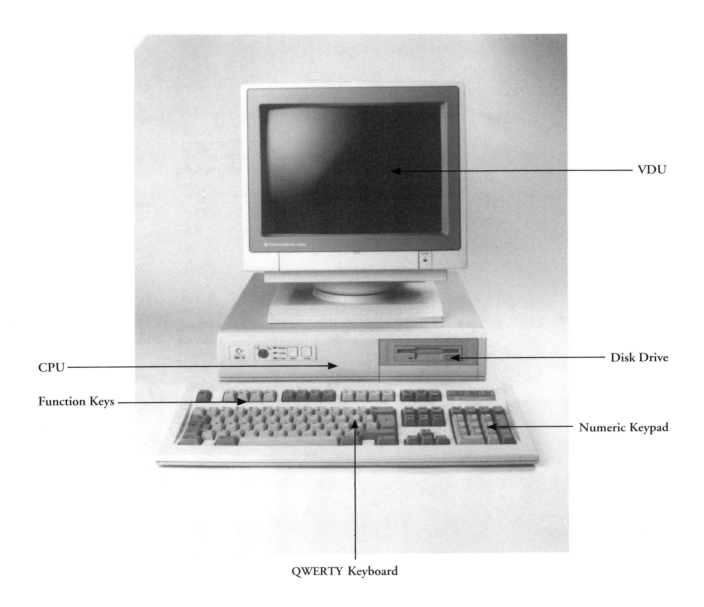

VDU

CPU

Disk Drive

Function Keys

Numeric Keypad

QWERTY Keyboard

An electronic typewriter

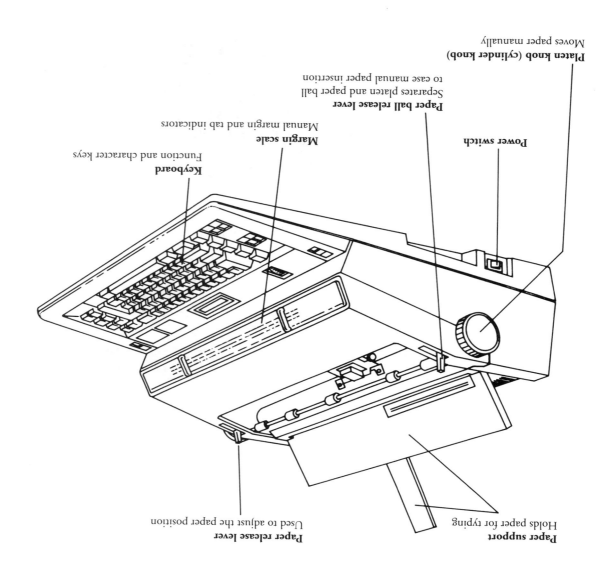

Keyboard
Function and character keys

Margin scale
Manual margin and tab indicators

Paper ball release lever
Separates platen and paper ball to ease manual paper insertion

Power switch

Platen knob (cylinder knob)
Moves paper manually

Paper release lever
Used to adjust the paper position

Paper support
Holds paper for typing

An electronic keyboard

The following diagram is typical of a computer keyboard, showing QWERTY keys, cursor movement keys, the function keys and the numeric keypad.

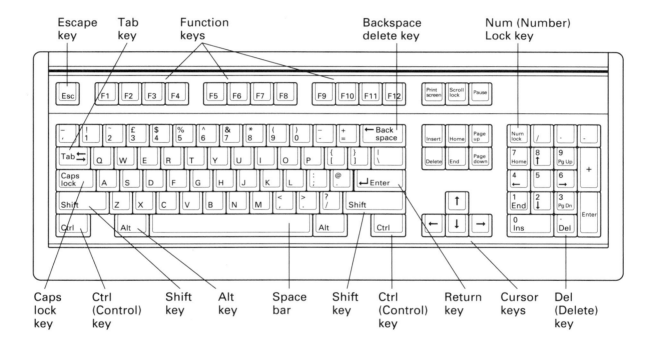

Basic machine parts

Typewriter

Paper Guide

Mark on paper rest which should be set at 0 prior to inserting the paper.

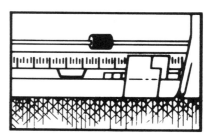

Linespace selector

Sets line spacing at 1, 1.5 and 2. Refer to manufacturer's handbook.

Margins

This is the border left and right, top and bottom on the page, beyond which text does not appear.

Standard settings are 1 inch for all margins.

Word processor

Paper Guide - Printer

A similar guide appears on dot matrix printers. The more sophisticated printers are free fed from a tray similar to that used for a photocopier.

Linespace selector

Located in your format menu.

Margins

Standard default settings are for 1 inch top and bottom, left and right.

Paper size

There are six vertical lines in every inch of text.

To set left and right margins you must know what pitch you are using:

- 10 pitch (PICA) gives you 10 characters to every 1 inch of text.
- 12 pitch (ELITE) gives you 12 characters to every 1 inch of text.

The majority of business documents are printed on A4 size paper and the character spaces for A4 are as follows:

- 10 pitch (PICA) = 82 characters edge to edge on the page
- 12 pitch (ELITE) = 100 characters edge to edge on the page

Margin settings therefore are:

- 10 pitch left margin 10; right margin 72
- 12 pitch left margin 12; right margin 88

Posture

Posture is of vital importance at all times - pay particular attention to the following.

o   The keyboard should be level with the front edge of your desk.

o   Centre yourself opposite the letter 'J'.

o   Position your fingers on the HOME KEYS

   A S D F   J K L ;

left fingers on ASDF and right on JKL; Strike the space bar with your right thumb.

o   Sit up straight with your two feet flat on the ground.

o   Ensure your back is straight, shoulders back, elbows close to your side and the wrists slightly curved.

While this posture may seem unnatural at first, it is important that you relax into this position.

Keep your eyes on the text you are keying.

To begin

Typewriter

Ensure the paper is inserted at 0 and is straight.

Set for single line spacing and set margins of 1 inch on either side.

Carriage return 7 times from top of the page to leave a top margin of 1 inch.

Word processor

Ensure you are looking directly at the screen.

If you are having difficulty with glare, adjust the screen or have a screen filter fitted.

Open a new document. The standard default settings are adequate. Ensure your cursor is at 0 (the cursor is the position indicator on the screen) but ensure that justification is turned off.

Keyboard

R E L A X curving your fingers slightly and place on the HOME KEYS as shown. We will begin with a blank keyboard and enter the characters as we learn them. We begin with the HOME KEYS as illustrated.

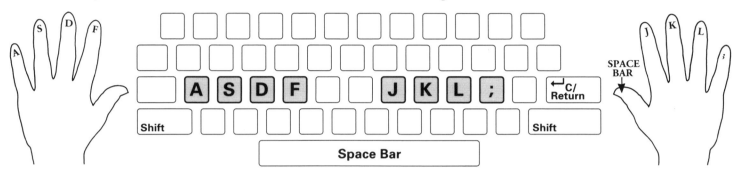

Slowly key a line of

A S D F ; L K J

Say each character to yourself as you key it.

If you are using a typewriter, a bell will sound as you reach the end of the line. You can key an additional 7 characters at this point. When you reach line end, stretch your little finger to the right and depress the Carriage Return key. DO NOT remove your hand from the keyboard.

If using a WP, the text will wraparound automatically from the end of one line to the beginning of the next.

Having keyed the first line, you must try not to look at the keys as you hit them. Place the book to the right or left of your keyboard, position your fingers correctly on the home keys and repeat the line.

This time ensure that your fingers remain on the home keys. It is from this base that you work to the top and bottom rows.

Key each line twice.

To get a space between the characters hit the space bar with your thumb.

```
ASDF;LKJ ASDF;LKJ ASDF;LKJ ASDF;LKJ ASDF;LKJ ASDF;LKJ
ASDF ;LKJ ASDF ;LKJ ASDF ;LKJ SDF ;LKJ ASDF ;LKJ ASDF

ALL ALL ALL ALL ALL ALL ALL ALL ALL ALL ALL ALL ALL ALL ALL
DAD DAD DAD DAD DAD DAD DAD DAD DAD DAD DAD DAD DAD DAD DAD
FAD FAD FAD FAD FAD FAD FAD FAD FAD FAD FAD FAD FAD FAD FAD

ALAS; ALAS; ALAS; ALAS; ALAS; ALAS; ALAS; ALAS; ALAS; ALAS;
FALL; FALL; FALL; FALL; FALL; FALL; FALL; FALL; FALL; FALL;
SALAD SALAD SALAD SALAD SALAD SALAD SALAD SALAD SALAD SALAD

AS SAD AS DAD; AS SAD AS DAD; AS SAD AS DAD; AS SAD AS DAD;
```

Refer to the users' manual for your machine or, alternatively, check with your tutor and set margins of 2 inches on either side for these drills.

Students have the option of keying text in either upper case (caps) or lower case. To obtain upper case, depress the shift lock but note that the semi-colon is a lower case character.

We recommend upper case for ease of proof-reading.

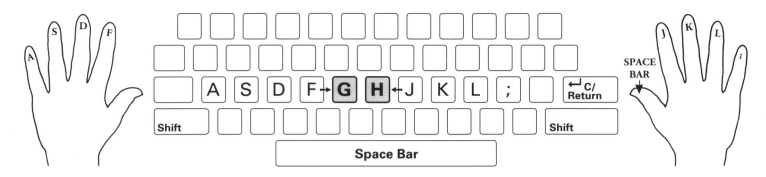

New key G (index finger left)

IMPORTANT When moving a finger from the home key YOU MUST return that finger to its home position before you hit the next character, eg in 'FLAGS' the index finger must be returned to the F before hitting the L.

Drill each line twice.

```
FGF FGF FGF FGF FGF FGF FGF FGF FGF FGF FGF FGF FGF FGF FGF
SAG SAG SAG SAG SAG SAG SAG SAG SAG SAG SAG SAG SAG SAG SAG

FLAGS FLAGS FLAGS FLAGS FLAGS FLAGS FLAGS FLAGS FLAGS FLAGS
ASKS; ASKS; ASKS; ASKS; ASKS; ASKS; ASKS; ASKS; ASKS; ASKS;
GLASS GLASS GLASS GLASS GLASS GLASS GLASS GLASS GLASS GLASS

A GAS SAGA;    A GAS SAGA;    A GAS SAGA;    A GAS SAGA;    A GAS SAGA;
ASK A LAD;    ASK A LAD;    ASK A LAD;    ASK A LAD;    ASK A LAD;
```

New key H (index finger right)

```
JHJ JHJ JHJ JHJ JHJ JHJ JHJ JHJ JHJ JHJ JHJ JHJ JHJ JHJ JHJ
HAD HAD HAD HAD HAD HAD HAD HAD HAD HAD HAD HAD HAD HAD HAD

GASH GASH GASH GASH GASH GASH GASH GASH GASH GASH GASH GASH
HASH HASH HASH HASH HASH HASH HASH HASH HASH HASH HASH HASH
SHALL SHALL SHALL SHALL SHALL SHALL SHALL SHALL SHALL SHALL
JAFFAS JAFFAS JAFFAS JAFFAS JAFFAS JAFFAS JAFFAS JAFFAS

A GLAD LASS ADDS A DASH; A GLAD LASS ADDS A DASH;
```

Feet
Flat
on
Floor

Well done! You have now finished the home keys. Progress to the next section but remember you must KEEP YOUR EYES ON THE TEXT, not on the keyboard.

Index

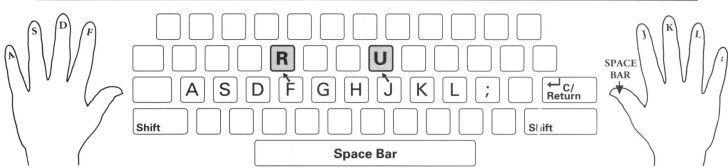

New key R (index finger left)

We are now moving from the home row using the index finger from F to R.

As each index finger is used for 6 keys, it is VITAL that you return to the home position each time.

Drill each line twice.

FRF   FRF   FRF   FRF   FRF   FRF   FRF   FRF   FRF   FRF   FRF   FRF   FRF   FRF
FAR   FAR   FAR   FAR   FAR   FAR   FAR   FAR   FAR   FAR   FAR   FAR   FAR   FAR
DARK DARK DARK DARK DARK DARK DARK DARK DARK DARK DARK

New key U (index finger right)

Remember to return to the home keys.

JUJ   JUJ   JUJ   JUJ   JUJ   JUJ   JUJ   JUJ   JUJ   JUJ   JUJ   JUJ   JUJ   JUJ
JUG   JUG   JUG   JUG   JUG   JUG   JUG   JUG   JUG   JUG   JUG   JUG   JUG   JUG
FULL FULL FULL FULL FULL FULL FULL FULL FULL FULL FULL

FURL FURL FURL FURL FURL FURL FURL FURL FURL FURL FURL
LARK LARK LARK LARK LARK LARK LARK LARK LARK LARK LARK
HUSK HUSK HUSK HUSK HUSK HUSK HUSK HUSK HUSK HUSK HUSK

LAUGH   LAUGH   LAUGH   LAUGH   LAUGH   LAUGH   LAUGH   LAUGH   LAUGH
SULKS   SULKS   SULKS   SULKS   SULKS   SULKS   SULKS   SULKS   SULKS

A   FULL   JUG   FALLS   A   FULL   JUG   FALLS   A   FULL   JUG   FALLS

Stretch Little Finger for C/Return - Do Not Remove from Home Keys

ZURICH ENTERPRISES PLC

Staff Pension Scheme

	1992 (12 months) IR£'000	1991 (18 months) IR£'000
INCOME		
Contributions received	1,330	2,397
Investment income	2,161	2,560
Other income	4	16
	3,495	4,973
OUTGOINGS		
Benefits	1,623	1,363
Other payments		
Life assurance premium	27	52
ADMINISTRATION COSTS		
Investment management charges	85	216
	1,735	1,631
GROSS INCREASE IN FUND	1,760	3,342
PENSION FUND LEVY	30	109
NET INCREASE IN FUND	1,730	3,233

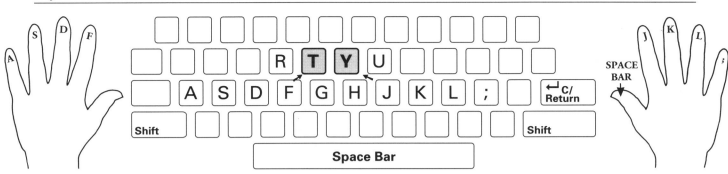

New key T (index finger left)

Stretch the index finger from F diagonally up to T and remember to

RETURN TO THE HOME KEYS.

Drill each line twice.

```
FRF  FTF  FRF  FTF  FRF  FTF  FRF  FTF  FRF  FTF  FRF  FTF  FRF  FTF
FAT  FAT  FAT  FAT  FAT  FAT  FAT  FAT  FAT  FAT  FAT  FAT  FAT  FAT
HAT  HAT  HAT  HAT  HAT  HAT  HAT  HAT  HAT  HAT  HAT  HAT  HAT  HAT
```

New key Y (index finger right)

Similar stretch as that for T.

```
JUJ  JYJ  JUJ  JYJ  JUJ  JYJ  JUJ  JYJ  JUJ  JYJ  JUJ  JYJ  JUJ  JYJ
TRY  TRY  TRY  TRY  TRY  TRY  TRY  TRY  TRY  TRY  TRY  TRY  TRY  TRY
STY  STY  STY  STY  STY  STY  STY  STY  STY  STY  STY  STY  STY  STY

RUTH  RUTH  RUTH  RUTH  RUTH  RUTH  RUTH  RUTH  RUTH  RUTH  RUTH
THAT  THAT  THAT  THAT  THAT  THAT  THAT  THAT  THAT  THAT  THAT
YARD  YARD  YARD  YARD  YARD  YARD  YARD  YARD  YARD  YARD  YARD

DARTS  DARTS  DARTS  DARTS  DARTS  DARTS  DARTS  DARTS  DARTS
STRAY  STRAY  STRAY  STRAY  STRAY  STRAY  STRAY  STRAY  STRAY

RUTH HAS A FUR HAT;    RUTH HAS A FUR HAT;
A FLUFFY RUG;    A FLUFFY RUG;    A FLUFFY RUG;    A FLUFFY RUG;
ASK SARAH;    ASK SARAH;    ASK SARAH;    ASK SARAH;    ASK SARAH;
ARTHUR SULKS;    ARTHUR SULKS;    ARTHUR SULKS;    ARTHUR SULKS;
```

C/Return Twice for a Free Line

BALANCE SHEET AS AT 31 OCTOBER 1992

Fixed Assets	Cost	Accumulated Depreciation	Net Book Value
	£	£	£
Premises	25,000	–	25,000
Machinery	18,000	1,800	16,200
Fixtures	6,000	–	6,000
Vehicles	9,000	–	9,000
	58,000	1,800	56,200

Current Assets

Stock		25,600	
Debtors		3,210	
Insurance prepaid		1,100	
		29,910	

Current Liabilities

Creditors	8,700		
Loan	5,000		
Expenses due	13,755		
Working Capital			2,455
Net Assets			58,645

Financed By

Capital	45,335		
Net Profit	14,710	60,045	
Drawings		1,400	
Capital Employed			58,645

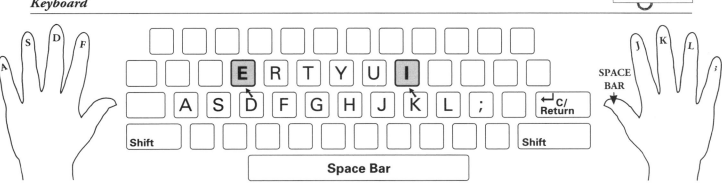

New key E (middle finger left)

When moving the middle fingers it is important that they are moved on their own and that the index and ring fingers do not travel with them. And always remember to

RETURN TO THE HOME KEYS.

Drill each line twice.

DED DED DED DED DED DED DED DED DED DED DED DED DED
DED DED LED LED LED LED LED LED LED LED LED LED LED
THE THE THE THE THE THE THE THE THE THE THE THE THE

New key I (middle finger right)

KIK KIK KIK KIK KIK KIK KIK KIK KIK KIK KIK KIK KIK
HIS HIS HIS HIS HIS HIS HIS HIS HIS HIS HIS HIS HIS
SIR SIR SIR SIR SIR SIR SIR SIR SIR SIR SIR SIR SIR

DEAL DEAL DEAL DEAL DEAL DEAL DEAL DEAL DEAL DEAL DEAL
GIRL GIRL GIRL GIRL GIRL GIRL GIRL GIRL GIRL GIRL GIRL
EASE EASE EASE EASE EASE EASE EASE EASE EASE EASE EASE
HIDE HIDE HIDE HIDE HIDE HIDE HIDE HIDE HIDE HIDE HIDE

DRILL DRILL DRILL DRILL DRILL DRILL DRILL DRILL DRILL
GUESS GUESS GUESS GUESS GUESS GUESS GUESS GUESS GUESS
FIELD FIELD FIELD FIELD FIELD FIELD FIELD FIELD FIELD

LUGGAGE LUGGAGE LUGGAGE LUGGAGE LUGGAGE LUGGAGE LUGGAGE

HE LIKES EGGS;   HE LIKES EGGS;   HE LIKES EGGS;
GET A RED RUG;   GET A RED RUG;   GET A RED RUG;
HIDE THE FILE;   HIDE THE FILE;   HIDE THE FILE;
THE LAD HAS DARK HAIR;   THE LAD HAS DARK HAIR;
FILL HIS GLASS;   FILL HIS GLASS;   FILL HIS GLASS;
THEY TRIED THE FRESH FRUIT;   THEY TRIED THE FRESH FRUIT;

> *Hit Space Bar Lightly with Right Thumb*

ZURICH ENTERPRISES plc
Staff Pension Plan

NET ASSET STATEMENT
As at 31 December 1992

		1992 IR£'000	1991 IR£'000
INVESTMENT ASSETS		44,710	38,427
CURRENT ASSETS	Tax refunds due	99	61
	Dividends receivable	383	258
	Cash deposits	2,146	15
	Interest receivable	12	- -
		47,350	38,761
LIABILITIES	Creditors	123	158
	Zurich Enterprises plc	48	93
	Pension Fund Levy	24	109
		195	360
NET ASSETS		47,155	38,401

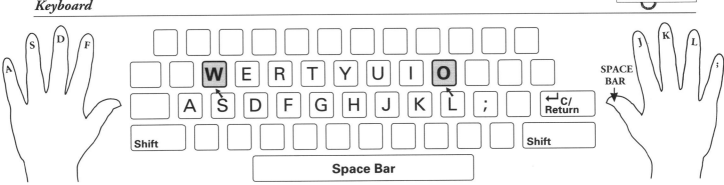

New key W (ring finger left)

You may find it necessary for this reach to move the little finger to the top row, but do try and stretch the ring fingers independently.

Drill each line twice.

```
SWS  SWS  SWS  SWS  SWS  SWS  SWS  SWS  SWS  SWS  SWS  SWS  SWS  SWS
WAS  WAS  WAS  WAS  WAS  WAS  WAS  WAS  WAS  WAS  WAS  WAS  WAS  WAS
FEW  FEW  FEW  FEW  FEW  FEW  FEW  FEW  FEW  FEW  FEW  FEW  FEW  FEW
```

New key O (ring finger right)

```
LOL  LOL  LOL  LOL  LOL  LOL  LOL  LOL  LOL  LOL  LOL  LOL  LOL  LOL
LOT  LOT  LOT  LOT  LOT  LOT  LOT  LOT  LOT  LOT  LOT  LOT  LOT  LOT
OLD  OLD  OLD  OLD  OLD  OLD  OLD  OLD  OLD  OLD  OLD  OLD  OLD  OLD

GREW  GREW  GREW  GREW  GREW  GREW  GREW  GREW  GREW  GREW  GREW
GOOD  GOOD  GOOD  GOOD  GOOD  GOOD  GOOD  GOOD  GOOD  GOOD  GOOD
WIFE  WIFE  WIFE  WIFE  WIFE  WIFE  WIFE  WIFE  WIFE  WIFE  WIFE
SLOW  SLOW  SLOW  SLOW  SLOW  SLOW  SLOW  SLOW  SLOW  SLOW  SLOW

THROW  THROW  THROW  THROW  THROW  THROW  THROW  THROW  THROW
HOUSE  HOUSE  HOUSE  HOUSE  HOUSE  HOUSE  HOUSE  HOUSE  HOUSE
WORLD  WORLD  WORLD  WORLD  WORLD  WORLD  WORLD  WORLD  WORLD

HOLDER  HOLDER  HOLDER  HOLDER  HOLDER  HOLDER  HOLDER  HOLDER
FLOWER  FLOWER  FLOWER  FLOWER  FLOWER  FLOWER  FLOWER  FLOWER

THERE WAS A FLAW WITH THE DRESS;
A WAITER FILLED THE JUG WITH WATER;
THE DRESS IS WHITE WITH RED FLOWERS;
GET THE LADY A SEAT;   GET THE LADY A SEAT;
THROW THE HOOK;    THROW THE HOOK;    THROW THE HOOK;
SELL THE GLASSES;    SELL THE GLASSES;    SELL THE GLASSES;
```

> # *Eyes on Text*

Say Each Character to Yourself as You Key It

TRADING, PROFIT AND LOSS ACCOUNT FOR YEAR ENDED 31 OCTOBER 1992

	£	£	£
Sales		41,000	
Returns		<u>1,500</u>	39,500
Opening stock		5,000	
Purchases	11,500		
Returns	<u>1,000</u>	10,500	
Carriage in		<u>480</u>	
Closing stock		10,980	<u>6,380</u>
Gross Profit		4,600	33,120
Discount received		420	
Bad debt recovered		<u>180</u>	<u>600</u>
Adjusted Gross Profit			33,720
Less Expenses			
Rent & Rates		4,000	
Light & Heat		1,000	
Insurance		1,300	
Bad debts		1,750	
Discount		240	
Post & Stationery		75	
Petrol		755	
Wages		4,900	
Packing expenses		330	
Repairs		560	
Carriage		150	
Advertising		1,200	
Telephone		350	
Bank Interest		500	
Bank Charges		100	
Depreciation		<u>1,800</u>	<u>19,010</u>
Net Profit			<u>14,710</u>

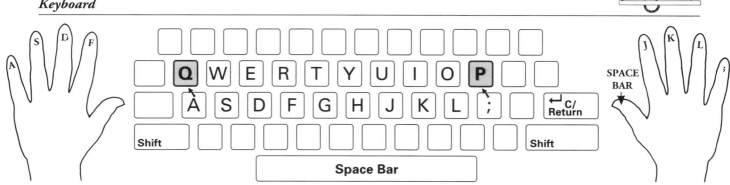

New key Q (little finger left)

AQA AQA AQA AQA AQA AQA AQA AQA AQA AQA AQA AQA AQA AQA
AQUA AQUA AQUA AQUA AQUA AQUA AQUA AQUA AQUA AQUA AQUA
QUIT QUIT QUIT QUIT QUIT QUIT QUIT QUIT QUIT QUIT QUIT
QUAY QUAY QUAY QUAY QUAY QUAY QUAY QUAY QUAY QUAY QUAY

New key P (little finger right)

;P; ;P; ;P; ;P; ;P; ;P; ;P; ;P; ;P; ;P; ;P; ;P; ;P; ;P;
PRAY PRAY PRAY PRAY PRAY PRAY PRAY PRAY PRAY PRAY PRAY
PART PART PART PART PART PART PART PART PART PART PART
POST POST POST POST POST POST POST POST POST POST POST

QUOTE QUOTE QUOTE QUOTE QUOTE QUOTE QUOTE QUOTE QUOTE
HAPPY HAPPY HAPPY HAPPY HAPPY HAPPY HAPPY HAPPY HAPPY

QUARTER QUARTER QUARTER QUARTER QUARTER QUARTER QUARTER
PREPARE PREPARE PREPARE PREPARE PREPARE PREPARE PREPARE

PLEASE WEIGH A QUARTER OF PEAS;
LISA LIKES HER SQUASH;   LISA LIKES HER SQUASH;
THE RAT SQUEALED ALOUD;   THE RAT SQUEALED ALOUD;
TAKE THE APPLE PIE WITH YOU;   TAKE THE APPLE PIE WITH YOU;
SHE TYPES HER LETTERS ON THE TYPEWRITER;   HE USES THE WORD PROCESSOR

Even, Rhythmic Strokes

One more to go! We will now begin the bottom (and final) row.
Before we do, check your posture:

SHOULDERS	Back and relaxed
BODY	Centred opposite 'J'
BACK	Sit erect, sloping slightly forward
FINGERS	Curved slightly over the keys
FEET	Flat on the floor
WRISTS	Slightly curved

Typing sums of money

When typing sums of money, make sure that all decimal points are under one another and all units, tens, hundreds, etc are also under each other.

If you are using a computer, set a decimal tab which will automatically align figures by the decimal point. If typing amounts without a decimal point, use the right align tab.

Ruling sums of money

£	
240.50	
1,240.00	
10.00	
8.00	no return
	return 2
1,498.50	return 1

To obtain the double underline, use the interliner. If using a computer you may have a double underscore facility, if not use the equals (=) sign ============

The following pages contain financial documents which will give you practice with the numeric keypad.

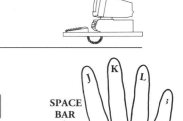

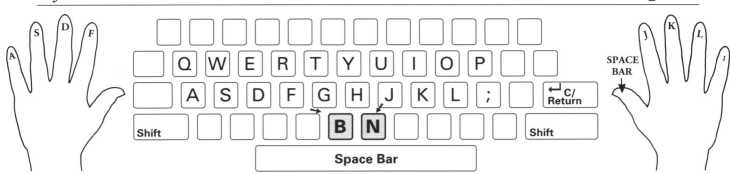

New key N (index finger right)

Moving this time from J to N. It is important, as always,
to RETURN TO THE HOME KEYS.

Drill each line twice.

```
JNJ  JNJ  JNJ  JNJ  JNJ  JNJ  JNJ  JNJ  JNJ  JNJ  JNJ  JNJ  JNJ  JNJ
TAN  TAN  TAN  TAN  TAN  TAN  TAN  TAN  TAN  TAN  TAN  TAN  TAN  TAN
AND  AND  AND  AND  AND  AND  AND  AND  AND  AND  AND  AND  AND  AND
HEN  HEN  HEN  HEN  HEN  HEN  HEN  HEN  HEN  HEN  HEN  HEN  HEN  HEN

NEAT  NEAT  NEAT  NEAT  NEAT  NEAT  NEAT  NEAT  NEAT  NEAT  NEAT
WANT  WANT  WANT  WANT  WANT  WANT  WANT  WANT  WANT  WANT  WANT
PLAN  PLAN  PLAN  PLAN  PLAN  PLAN  PLAN  PLAN  PLAN  PLAN  PLAN

ANNUAL  ANNUAL  ANNUAL  ANNUAL  ANNUAL  ANNUAL  ANNUAL  ANNUAL
NOTION  NOTION  NOTION  NOTION  NOTION  NOTION  NOTION  NOTION
```

New key B (index finger left)

> # Wrists and Arms Straight - Fingers Curved

```
FBF  FBF  FBF  FBF  FBF  FBF  FBF  FBF  FBF  FBF  FBF  FBF  FBF  FBF
TAB  TAB  TAB  TAB  TAB  TAB  TAB  TAB  TAB  TAB  TAB  TAB  TAB  TAB
BOY  BOY  BOY  BOY  BOY  BOY  BOY  BOY  BOY  BOY  BOY  BOY  BOY  BOY
BUT  BUT  BUT  BUT  BUT  BUT  BUT  BUT  BUT  BUT  BUT  BUT  BUT  BUT

BANK  BANK  BANK  BANK  BANK  BANK  BANK  BANK  BANK  BANK  BANK
BUSY  BUSY  BUSY  BUSY  BUSY  BUSY  BUSY  BUSY  BUSY  BUSY  BUSY
ABLE  ABLE  ABLE  ABLE  ABLE  ABLE  ABLE  ABLE  ABLE  ABLE  ABLE

BUSINESS  BUSINESS  BUSINESS  BUSINESS  BUSINESS  BUSINESS
NEIGHBOUR  NEIGHBOUR  NEIGHBOUR  NEIGHBOUR  NEIGHBOUR
LIBRARIAN  LIBRARIAN  LIBRARIAN  LIBRARIAN  LIBRARIAN

PENELOPE  WAS  HER  GOOD  FRIEND
SHE  WAS  WRONG  WITH  HER  ANSWER
AFTER  THE  FIRE  THE  NEIGHBOURS  WERE  ALL  HELPFUL
THEY  BEGAN  THEIR  SKIING  LESSONS  ON  THE  DRY  SLOPE
LINDA  WAS  A  HAPPY  PERSON;  LINDA  WAS  A  HAPPY  PERSON;
THE  BUSINESS  WAS  GOING  WELL  AND  THE  PROFIT  WAS  UP  ON  LAST  YEAR
```

Middle finger, keys 2, 5, 8

555	888	222	555	888	222
258	852	258	558	825	285
5555	8888	2222	2585	5852	8528
2852	8582	5228	5825	5228	5282

Ring finger, keys 3, 6, 9

666	999	333	666	999	333
369	963	369	336	639	933
6666	9999	3333	3696	6963	9639
3963	6993	3996	6339	9369	6936

Thumb is used for 0

000	001	002	003	004	005
006	007	008	009	300	320
210	560	890	740	780	501

Combination keys for practice

450	631	879	900	824	655
452	760	890	200	113	687
1029	5160	3481	5387	9102	3847
2234	9873	2938	4929	3142	8472

If you can use the numeric keypad efficiently you will speed up your entry time for figures.

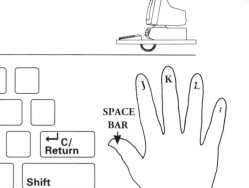

New key M (index finger right)

Stretching back from J to M.

JMJ JMJ JMJ JMJ JMJ JMJ JMJ JMJ JMJ JMJ JMJ JMJ JMJ JMJ
HIM HIM HIM HIM HIM HIM HIM HIM HIM HIM HIM HIM HIM HIM
SUM SUM SUM SUM SUM SUM SUM SUM SUM SUM SUM SUM SUM SUM
MEN MEN MEN MEN MEN MEN MEN MEN MEN MEN MEN MEN MEN MEN

NEAT NEAT NEAT NEAT NEAT NEAT NEAT NEAT NEAT NEAT NEAT
MEAL MEAL MEAL MEAL MEAL MEAL MEAL MEAL MEAL MEAL MEAL
THEM THEM THEM THEM THEM THEM THEM THEM THEM THEM THEM
GAME GAME GAME GAME GAME GAME GAME GAME GAME GAME GAME

MONEY MONEY MONEY MONEY MONEY MONEY MONEY MONEY MONEY
MINUTES MINUTES MINUTES MINUTES MINUTES MINUTES MINUTES
MISTAKE MISTAKE MISTAKE MISTAKE MISTAKE MISTAKE MISTAKE

New key V (index finger left)

FVF FVF FVF FVF FVF FVF FVF FVF FVF FVF FVF FVF FVF FVF
VET VET VET VET VET VET VET VET VET VET VET VET VET VET
VAN VAN VAN VAN VAN VAN VAN VAN VAN VAN VAN VAN VAN VAN

VERY VERY VERY VERY VERY VERY VERY VERY VERY VERY VERY
ABOVE ABOVE ABOVE ABOVE ABOVE ABOVE ABOVE ABOVE ABOVE
NEVER NEVER NEVER NEVER NEVER NEVER NEVER NEVER NEVER

REMOVE REMOVE REMOVE REMOVE REMOVE REMOVE REMOVE REMOVE
VOLUME VOLUME VOLUME VOLUME VOLUME VOLUME VOLUME VOLUME

PROOF READ YOUR WORK VERY WELL
REMOVE THE VEHICLE FROM THE ROAD
VALERIE VOWED NEVER TO TELL ANYBODY
FIVE BRAVE PEOPLE WERE SAVED BY THE DOG
THE MINUTES OF THE MONTHLY MEETING WERE READ
NEVER LEAVE ANY TYPEWRITING ERRORS UNCORRECTED
I NEED THE REPORT ON MY DESK FIRST THING TOMORROW MORNING

Check Your Posture

Fingers on the Home Keys

For use on computer keyboard only

Like the alphabetic keyboard the numeric keypad has a home position—4, 5, 6, on the middle row. Position your index finger on the 4, middle finger on 5 and ring finger on 6.

To use the numeric keypad you must turn on the numlock otherwise the cursor movement keys are the ones that function.

If you are keying text in several columns, set dec tabs or right aligned key, whichever is more appropriate to the work you are doing.

Drill the home row, keys 4, 5, 6

444	555	666	444	555	666
456	654	456	465	546	645
4444	5555	6666	4545	5656	4564
6464	5656	5454	4545	4646	6565

Bottom row, keys 1, 2, 3

Remember you MUST return your fingers to the home row after depressing each key.

111	222	333	111	222	333
123	321	123	213	132	312
1111	2222	3333	1232	3212	3123
3131	2323	2121	1313	3232	1212

Top row, keys 7, 8, 9

777	888	999	777	888	999
789	987	789	989	797	879
7777	8888	9999	7878	8989	7878
9797	8987	8798	7978	9898	9978

Are Your Fingers on the Home Row?

Index finger, keys 1, 4, 7

444	777	111	444	777	111
147	741	147	114	441	714
1111	4444	7777	1414	1717	1417
1774	4714	7147	1741	7471	4117

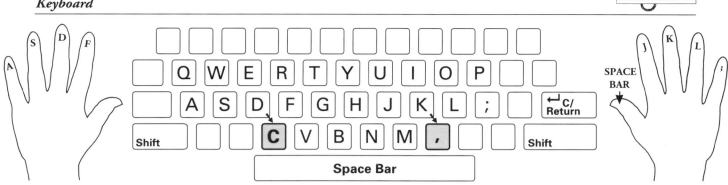

New key C (middle finger left)

Moving from D down to C.

DCD DCD DCD DCD DCD DCD DCD DCD DCD DCD DCD DCD DCD DCD
COD COD COD COD COD COD COD COD COD COD COD COD COD COD
ICE ICE ICE ICE ICE ICE ICE ICE   ICE   ICE ICE ICE   ICE ICE
COP COP COP COP COP COP COP COP COP COP COP COP COP COP

CAME CAME CAME CAME CAME CAME CAME CAME CAME CAME CAME
FACT FACT FACT FACT FACT FACT FACT FACT FACT FACT FACT
CAKE CAKE CAKE CAKE CAKE CAKE CAKE CAKE CAKE CAKE CAKE

TOUCH TOUCH TOUCH TOUCH TOUCH TOUCH TOUCH TOUCH TOUCH
COMBINE COMBINE COMBINE COMBINE COMBINE COMBINE COMBINE
ACHIEVE ACHIEVE ACHIEVE ACHIEVE ACHIEVE ACHIEVE ACHIEVE

, (comma, middle finger right)

Some typewriters do not have the comma as an upper case character. If that is the case, release the shift lock and type this exercise in the lower case.

K,K K,K K,K K,K K,K K,K K,K K,K K,K K,K K,K K,K K,K K,K,
JANUARY, FEBRUARY, MARCH, APRIL, MAY, JUNE, JULY, AUGUST,
SEPTEMBER, OCTOBER, NOVEMBER, DECEMBER

MONDAY, TUESDAY, WEDNESDAY, THURSDAY, FRIDAY, SATURDAY, SUNDAY

THE COUNCIL SAT ONCE EVERY QUARTER
HER JACKET WAS BLACK, WHITE AND RED
THE CHIEF CHATTED CALMLY TO HIS FORCE
COME TO THE CAVES AND BRING THE COCONUTS
THE LOCAL DENTIST HAD A THRIVING PRACTICE
PRACTISE THE KEYBOARD EVERY DAY TO ACHIEVE SUCCESS
THERE WAS A CHOICE OF THREE FLAVOURS, CHOCOLATE, VANILLA, AND STRAWBERRY

Feet Flat on Floor

Exercise 9

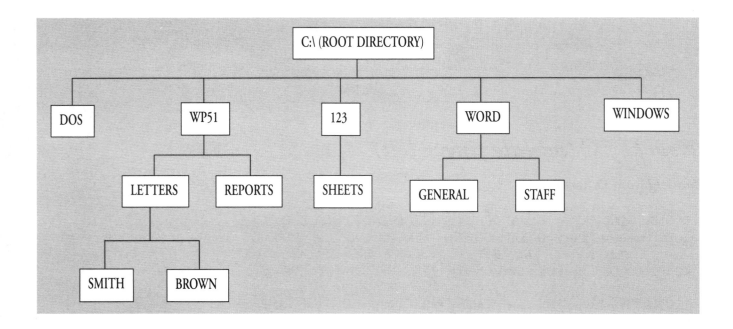

Exercise 10

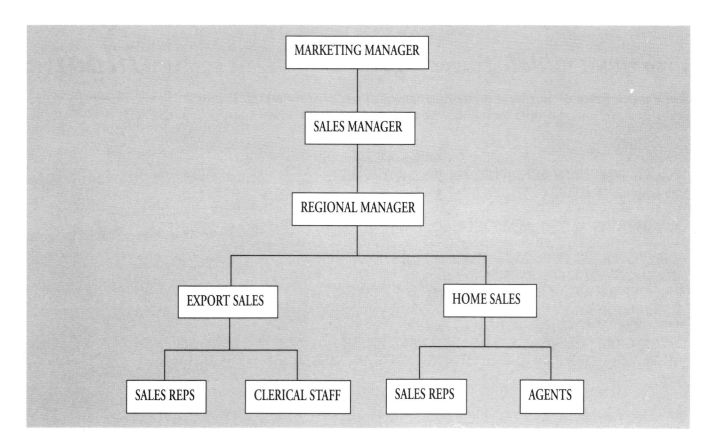

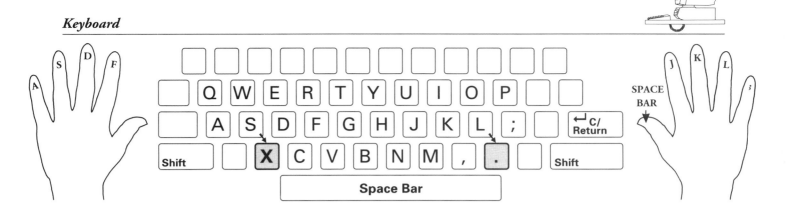

New key X (ring finger left)

Quite a difficult reach, as with the W it may be necessary to move the middle finger slightly.

SXS   SXS   SXS   SXS   SXS   SXS   SXS   SXS   SXS   SXS   SXS   SXS   SXS   SXS
SIX   SIX   SIX   SIX   SIX   SIX   SIX   SIX   SIX   SIX   SIX   SIX   SIX   SIX
TAX   TAX   TAX   TAX   TAX   TAX   TAX   TAX   TAX   TAX   TAX   TAX   TAX   TAX
WAX   WAX   WAX   WAX   WAX   WAX   WAX   WAX   WAX   WAX   WAX   WAX   WAX   WAX

EXIT   EXIT   EXIT   EXIT   EXIT   EXIT   EXIT   EXIT   EXIT   EXIT   EXIT
EXAM   EXAM   EXAM   EXAM   EXAM   EXAM   EXAM   EXAM   EXAM   EXAM   EXAM
TEXT   TEXT   TEXT   TEXT   TEXT   TEXT   TEXT   TEXT   TEXT   TEXT   TEXT
INDEX   INDEX   INDEX   INDEX   INDEX   INDEX   INDEX   INDEX   INDEX
EXAMPLES   EXAMPLES   EXAMPLES   EXAMPLES   EXAMPLES   EXAMPLES
MAXIMUM MAXIMUM MAXIMUM MAXIMUM MAXIMUM MAXIMUM MAXIMUM

> # Fingers on the Home Keys

. (fullstop, ring finger right)

Some typewriters do not have the fullstop as an upper case character.
If that is the case, release the shift lock and type this exercise in the lower case.

L.L L.L L.L L.L L.L L.L L.L L.L L.L L.L L.L L.L L.L L.L

THE TAX BILL WAS VERY HIGH.
THE MAXIMUM AGE LEVEL WAS TWENTY SIX.
THEY STAYED IN A FIVE STAR HOTEL AND IT WAS LUXURIOUS.
IF YOU CANNOT FIND THE CORRECT PAGE THEN CHECK THE INDEX.
HIS EXAMINATION RESULTS WERE EXCELLENT THIS YEAR, OF COURSE
HE DID STUDY HARD.
THE LECTURER GAVE EXTRA EXAMPLES AND EXACT ANSWERS WHICH
HELPED EXPLAIN THE TEXT TO THE STUDENTS.

Exercise 8

MULDOWNEY MOTORS
Mill Street, Tralee, Co Kerry

YEAR	MAKE	COLOUR	MILEAGE	PRICE £
1992	Ford XR2i	Black	19 000	8 950
1992	BMW 316i	Silver	19 000	15 500
1992	Fiat Tempra	Green	10 000	9 900
1991	Vanette LWB	Red	20 000	6 950
1991	Maxima	Gold	17 500	17 500
1991	Renault 19 Supervan	White	28 000	7 950
1991	Mercedes 300 E	Gold	64 000	27 000
1990	Nissan 200 ZX	Blue	60 000	13 500
1990	Mazda 626 Diesel	Silver	99 000	10 050

All makes of new and used cars sold
Finance arranged on premises, if required

Flow charts

An organisation or flow chart shows the various structures and departments in a business. It can also be used to illustrate the flow and direction of information.

o   Centre the longest line in the chart leaving an equal amount of space between each group, eg 3/5/7 spaces.

o   Centre each horizontal line.

o   Centre the chart vertically on the page.

o   Complete all lines and boxes neatly with black pen.

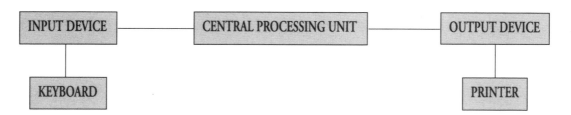

Key the Charts on the Following Page, Ruling as Shown

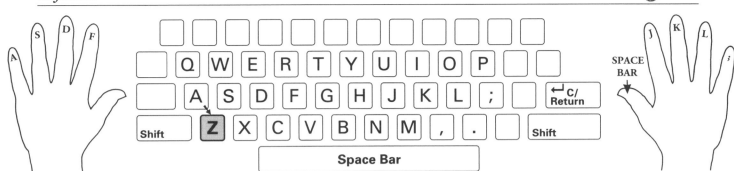

New key Z (little finger left)

AZA AZA AZA AZA AZA AZA AZA AZA AZA AZA AZA AZA AZA AZA
ZAP ZAP ZAP ZAP ZAP ZAP ZAP ZAP ZAP ZAP ZAP ZAP ZAP ZAP
ZOO ZOO ZOO ZOO ZOO ZOO ZOO ZOO ZOO ZOO ZOO ZOO ZOO ZOO
ZIP ZIP ZIP ZIP ZIP ZIP ZIP ZIP ZIP ZIP ZIP ZIP ZIP ZIP

LAZE LAZE LAZE LAZE LAZE LAZE LAZE LAZE LAZE LAZE LAZE
FIZZY FIZZY FIZZY FIZZY FIZZY FIZZY FIZZY FIZZY FIZZY
AMAZE AMAZE AMAZE AMAZE AMAZE AMAZE AMAZE AMAZE AMAZE
ZEALOUS ZEALOUS ZEALOUS ZEALOUS ZEALOUS ZEALOUS ZEALOUS
SQUEEZE SQUEEZE SQUEEZE SQUEEZE SQUEEZE SQUEEZE SQUEEZE

SHE LOVED JAZZ MUSIC.
PUT YOUR TYPING PAPER IN AT ZERO.
THE ROCKET ZOOMED UPWARDS TO THE SKY.
HE WAS ALWAYS LATE AND SO THEY WERE AMAZED TO SEE THAT HE HAD ARRIVED BEFORE THEM.
THE ORGANIZATION WAS LARGE BUT EACH DEPARTMENT WAS DIVIDED INTO SMALLER SIZES.

> **Well done! You have mastered the keyboard and can now progress to sentences and paragraphs.**

When you type everything in upper case (capitals) you can set the shift lock. But usually capitals are used at the beginning of sentences and to give emphasis to text. These INITIAL CAPITALS ARE OBTAINED BY HOLDING DOWN THE SHIFT KEY WITH THE OPPOSITE HAND to the one hitting the key.

For example if you wish to hit a capital R, you hold the shift key down with the little finger of the right hand as you hit the key. If you wish to have a capital U, hold the shift key down with the little finger of the left hand while you strike the key.

Leinster House, Kildare Steet, Dublin
The Golden Pages is a useful Data Bank of information.
Treasa and Celia run Donnybrook Creche in Morehampton Road.
Zenith Dry Cleaners have a collection service in Rathfarnham.
Bord Trachtala's head office is situated in Dublin at Merrion Hall, Strand Road in Sandymount.

Input the following exercises, ruling as shown.

Exercise 6

AN BORD TRACHTALA		
OFFICE	TELEPHONE	ADDRESS
DUBLIN	(01) 2695011	Merrion Hall, Sandymount, Dublin 2
CORK	(021) 271251/271252	67/69 South Mall, Cork
GALWAY	(091) 56600/1/2	Mervue Industrial Estate, Galway
LIMERICK	(061) 419811/419908	The Granary, Michael Street, Limerick
SLIGO	(071) 69477/69478	Finisklin Industrial Estate, Sligo
WATERFORD	(051) 78577	Industrial Estate, Cork Road, Waterford

Exercise 7

MORTGAGE RATES			
Lending Institute	Endow	Annuity	Monthly Cost per £000
ACC Bank	11.25	11.25	10.43
Allied Irish Banks	11.20	11.80	NA
Bank of Ireland	11.35	11.85	10.83
EBS Building Society	10.75	10.75	10.29
First National Building Society	10.99	10.99	10.45
ICS Building Society	11.45	11.45	10.77
Irish Life Building Society	11.45	11.20	10.60
Irish Nationwide Building Society	11.70	11.25	NA
Irish Permanent Building Society	11.20	11.16	10.43
Midland & Western Building Society	12.00	11.01	NA
National Irish Bank	11.25	11.25	10.42
Norwich Irish Building Society	11.95	11.95	11.12
TSB Bank	11.11	11.20	10.45
Ulster Bank	11.50	11.50	10.81

Rules of punctuation—spacing

NO   **SPACE before the apostrophe**
     eg Yvonne's typewriter has a line draw facility

NO   **SPACE within quotation marks or brackets**
     eg Your article in the "Irish Times" (Friday's edition) was well written

NO   **SPACE before or after a hyphen**
     eg Part-time staff do not receive luncheon vouchers

NO   **SPACE before or after punctuation marks in figure work**
     eg £25.08   10,000   13.30 pm

NO   **SPACES within the characters used to form an acronym**
     eg NATO, UNESCO, DART

Leave   **ONE SPACE after a comma, semi-colon; or colon:**

Leave   **ONE SPACE after an abbreviation within a sentence**
     eg Contact Robert Mitchell & Co Ltd

Leave   **ONE SPACE after initial letters preceding surnames**
     eg Miss R P McConnell

Leave   **ONE SPACE before and after a hyphen symbol when it is used as a dash**
     eg Bring an umbrella – it may rain

Leave   **TWO SPACES after a full-stop . a question mark ? or an exclamation mark ! at the end of a sentence.**
     eg Thank you for your letter. It was very nice to hear from you after such
     a long time! Perhaps we can meet and have lunch together soon?

Up to now your keyboarding has been confined to drilling words and word combinations. As you now begin to copy type you should note the following:

- Posture is as important now as it was in the early stages, and so is the need to KEEP YOUR FINGERS ON THE HOME KEYS.

- As you can no longer predict what character is coming next, your input speed will decrease; expect this to happen and be patient with it.

- Try to develop an easy, rhythmic touch, saying each character to yourself as you key it. Resist the temptation to hit quickly the characters you are familiar with as you will hesitate over the other keys and this will impair your speed development.

- It is sufficient to key each of these sentences once.

Alphabetic sentences

Zoe packed five of the bags with six liquid drinks. She did the job quickly and has finished all of her work.

Flexible working hours are requested by most employees as they can avoid rush hour traffic. John gets home quickly by taking the free zone.

They quickly placed all the boxes in rows. There were dozens of boxes containing all kinds of very expensive items from jugs to furs.

They organized their work efficiently and quickly and seized the opportunity to go home early. Everybody expected Jeff to be late.

There are just two columns in this exercise. Note how the title is lined flush with the left margin.

Exercise 3

SWORDS – ROUTE 41X
Timetable

<u>Morning Depart</u>

Glassmore (Terminus Route 41)	08.00
Rathbeale Road	
Taylor's Swords Village	08.03
Swords Main St	
Pinnock Hill	08.07

<u>Operates non-stop to</u>

Parnell Sq East, O'Connell St,
D'Olier St, Nassau St, Kildare St,
St Stephen's Green

<u>Evening Depart</u>

College of Surgeons	17.30
Dawson St	17.32
Suffolk St	17.33
Eden Quay	17.40
Lower Gardiner St	17.42

<u>Operates non-stop to</u>

Pinnock Hill, Swords Main St,
Taylor's Swords Village,
Rathbeale Road,
Glassmore (Terminus Route 41)

Input this exercise. Note that the column heading is treated as part of the column and that 'class' is the longest word in column 1.

Exercise 4

INFORMATION TECHNOLOGY
Teacher: Jim McIntyre

M O N D A Y

<u>Class</u>	<u>Time</u>	<u>Module</u>
A1	9.00 – 10.00	Spreadsheets
C3	10.00 – 11.00	DBase
A2	11.00 – 12.00	Spreadsheets
	L U N C H	
C2	13.00 – 14.00	Word Processing
A3	14.00 – 15.00	DBase

Key this exercise on A5 landscape leaving 3 spaces between each column.

Exercise 5

ADULT COMMUNITY LEARNING
<u>Programme 1994 – 1995</u>

<u>Evening</u>	<u>Time</u>	<u>Subject</u>
Monday	7.30 – 9.30	Basic electronics
Monday	7.00 – 9.30	Welding
Tuesday	7.00 – 9.00	Car maintenance
Tuesday	7.30 – 9.30	Radio theory
Wednesday	7.00 – 9.30	Morse code
Wednesday	7.00 – 9.30	Metalwork

RULING neatly can really enhance the appearance of a document. Follow the instructions below.

Horizontal method

– Draw an unbroken line from margin to margin.
– Leave one clear line before keying the heading (carriage return twice).
– Input your line and carriage return once.
– Draw your line, carriage return twice and continue typing.

Remember !!!!!

Turn up ONCE before and TWICE after each line.

Vertical ruling

This may be done with a black pen. Make sure all angles meet neatly. If using a computer you may have a line draw facility.

The following exercises are very good for speed development and are something you should constantly refer back to when trying to increase your speed. They can also be used at the start of each session as a warm-up. Type exactly as shown.

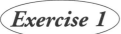

Exercise 1

The staff received a summer bonus.
In spite of herself she felt guilty.
Rush hour traffic is very stressful.
Please send me a copy of your brochure.

The restaurant is booked in your name.
The school rugby team won the cup this year.
You will find peace and quiet in the library.
A word processor eliminates repetitive typing.

Ten pitch machines fit ten characters to every inch.
The contract will be sent to you for your signature.
Fire drills are a very important part of fire safety.
Remember to check the expiry date on your credit card.

You will probably have discovered that your line endings differ from those in the book. An excessively uneven right-hand margin is most unattractive and you will find it necessary to divide words at line end if this is to be avoided.

There are some basic rules of word division which it is important that you understand and implement. Excessive word division, however, disrupts the flow of the text and should be avoided.

DIVIDE
- **always with the pronunciation of the word**
  eg prop-erty NOT pro-perty
- **after a prefix and before a suffix**
  eg com-bine, inter-view, men-tion, writ-ing
- **compound words at the point of division**
  eg week-end, flexi-time, time-table
- **when a consonant is doubled, divide between the two**
  eg accom-modate, ship-ping,
  Except if the root word ends in a double consonant
  eg miss-ing,
- **according to syllables**
  eg con-tact, men-tion

NEVER DIVIDE
- **proper names**
  eg Rathkeale, Midleton, Robinson
- **after an initial one-letter syllable**
  eg a-head, a-gain
- **sums of money IR£2,356.33 and numbers 77,089**
- **acronyms** eg NATO, UNESCO, DART
- **foreign words, unless you know the language and where to divide**
- **the last word in a paragraph or on a page**

Keeping these rules of word division in mind, key each of the following paragraphs once.

Key the following exercise allowing 3 spaces between each column. Set the shift lock for capitals.

Exercise 1

'C' FOR CAR

CAR ALARMS	CAR DEALERS	CAR HIRE
CAR PARTS	CAR 'PHONES	CAR STEREOS
CLUTCHES	COACHES	REPAIRS

Now that you are familiar with the technique, let's do a longer tab. Set your line space indicator for 1.5 and key the following. Note the use of spaced capitals and capitals for the main and sub-headings. This document would look better on A4 portrait.

Exercise 2

DUBLIN THEATRES

THEATRE	ADDRESS	TEL
Abbey & Peacock Theatres	Lr Abbey Street, Dublin 1	787222
Andrews Lane Theatre	9 - 16 Andrew's Lane, Dublin 2	6795720
Eblana Theatre	Busaras, Store Street, Dublin 1	6798404
Focus Theatre	6 Pembroke Place, Dublin 2	763071
Gaiety Theatre	South King Street, Dublin 2	771717
Gate Theatre	1 Cavendish Row, Dublin 1	744045
Lambert Puppet Theatre	Monkstown, Co Dublin	2800974
Olympia Theatre	72 Dame Steet, Dublin 2	777744
Project Arts Theatre	39 Essex Street East, Dublin 2	712321
Tivoli Theatre	Francis Street, Dublin 8	535998

You must book tickets directly with theatres, although Brown Thomas on Grafton Street take bookings for certain theatres.

Exercise 2

	STROKES	WORDS
Staff working for the same firm or organisation use memo forms to	66	13
communicate with each other in writing.	105	21
Some envelopes have a transparent section through which can be seen	71	14
the name and address of the addressee.	106	21
Papers are normally placed in date order within files; another name for	71	14
this type of order is chronological.	109	21
Recycling paper saves energy. Newspapers are classed as low grade	66	13
paper, but are the easiest to recycle.	105	21

How to calculate speed

If reading word count, divide by the number of minutes you were keying for.

If reading strokes at line end, then divide by five (to convert to words) and by the number of minutes you were typing for.

Example:

Ten minute speed test with a final stroke count of 1221.

Divide by 5 to convert strokes to words (244) and then by length of speed test (10 minutes) = 24 words per minute

For these exercises margins of 1 inch should be set on either side.

12 PITCH SETTINGS = 12/88
10 PITCH SETTINGS = 10/72

Accuracy Check – Ring Each Error in Pen

Exercise 3

	STROKES	WORDS
Office waste can be of a medium quality if free from	53	10
contamination such as plastics, metals, etc. Offices	107	21
could, without too much difficulty, make significant	160	32
contributions to recycling paper with the co-operation of	218	43
staff.	225	45
Irish towns and villages have a well-earned reputation	280	56
for the quality of their shopfronts, in terms of design	336	67
and craftsmanship. Shopfronts give distinction to buildings and add	387	77
to the attractiveness of streets.	439	88
If you have an old shopfront it is worth making every	493	99
effort to retain it, since you possess something which is	551	110
distinctive, perhaps rare or unique. It can add to the	607	121
interest of your shop, thereby increasing the potential	663	132
to attract customers.	685	137

(ENFO - Action Sheet 15)

Tabulation and Financial Work

We have already seen how the tab key is used to move quickly across the page to pre-set points.

But, firstly, please note the following:

o Ensure the paper is inserted at 0.

o Clear all margins and tabs. If you are working on a computer you will have pre-set tabs every 5 spaces; clear these.

o Check and know the pitch of your machine and the width of your page.

There are a number of methods that can be used for tab calculation. We have chosen the simplest form. Before typing, decide on the number of spaces you want to leave between columns. A common choice would be 3 or 5, depending on the width of the text.

This list of towns and villages is typed in 12 pitch on A5 landscape = 100 character spaces

TOWNS & VILLAGES		
Abbeydorney	Ballina	Cahir
Abbeyfeale	Ballincollig	Cahirciveen
Abbeyleix	Ballybofey	Cappawhite

o **Count the number of characters in your longest word or word combination in each vertical column. For example, in the exercise above Abbeydorney (11), Ballincollig (12) and Cahirciveen (11) are the longest words; to this amount you add the number of spaces between each column, ie 3.**

Character spaces   11 + 12 + 11 = 34
Spacing between columns x 2 columns = 6
Total   = 40
Subtract from page width 100 – 40 = 60 spaces to be divided between left and right margin
60 – 2 = 30

o Set your left margin at 30 and key Abbeydorney.
o Hit the space bar 3 times to give the spacing between columns and set the tab at this point.
o Key Ballina but note that this word is 5 spaces shorter than the longest word, so in addition to tapping the space bar 3 times for the width between the columns, you must also include these 5 spaces. Set the tab for the last column.
o Type Cahir and carriage return twice to leave 1 clear line space between the first and second line.
o Key Abbeyfeale and hit the tab key; key Ballincollig and hit the tab key; key Cahirciveen and carriage return.

Figure row

If your keyboard does not have the figure 1 or 0, then use letter l for one and a capital O for zero.

If using a computer you will also have a numeric keypad—see Chapter 7 for more details.

Work through each number until you feel confident with it.

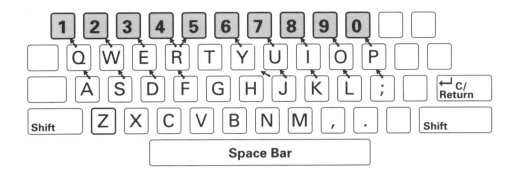

figure 1

AQ1	AQ1	AQ1	AQ1	AQ1	AQ1	AQ1	AQ1	AQ1	AQ1	AQ1	AQ1
Q1A	Q1A	Q1A	Q1A	Q1A	Q1A	Q1A	Q1A	Q1A	Q1A	Q1A	Q1A

figure 2

SW2	SW2	SW2	SW2	SW2	SW2	SW2	SW2	SW2	SW2	SW2	SW2
W2S	W2S	W2S	W2S	W2S	W2S	W2S	W2S	W2S	W2S	W2S	W2S

figure 3

DE3	DE3	DE3	DE3	DE3	DE3	DE3	DE3	DE3	DE3	DE3	DE3
E3D	E3D	E3D	E3D	E3D	E3D	E3D	E3D	E3D	E3D	E3D	E3D

figure 4

FR4	FR4	FR4	FR4	FR4	FR4	FR4	FR4	FR4	FR4	FR4	FR4
R4F	R4F	R4F	R4F	R4F	R4F	R4F	R4F	R4F	R4F	R4F	R4F

figure 5

FR5	FR5	FR5	FR5	FR5	FR5	FR5	FR5	FR5	FR5	FR5	FR5
R5F	R5F	R5F	R5F	R5F	R5F	R5F	R5F	R5F	R5F	R5F	R5F

figure 6

JY6	JY6	JY6	JY6	JY6	JY6	JY6	JY6	JY6	JY6	JY6	JY6
Y6J	Y6J	Y6J	Y6J	Y6J	Y6J	Y6J	Y6J	Y6J	Y6J	Y6J	Y6J

> *Use Home Keys as a Base and Stretch to Top Line Numerals*

Display the following advertisements on A5 portrait. Centre both horizontally and vertically.

FITZSIMONS UPHOLSTERY

Don't give it away
– We'll upholster it today

– oOo –

All Chesterfield suites, fireside chairs, antiques
Office furniture
Re-covered better than new

Handmade suites made to order

– oOo –

ALL MATERIALS FLAME RETARDANT

Tel (0506) 345678

WONGS CHINESE RESTAURANT
specialists in Cantonese & Szechuan

Monday – Thursday 6.00 pm – 12.00 am
Friday – Sunday 6.00 pm – 01.30 am

WE OFFER SPECIAL RATES FOR PARTIES

Excellent food at affordable prices
1 Crowe Street, Cork
Tel (021) 569265

Compose your own advertisement on both A4 and A5 paper for insertion in a local
newspaper. In one, give details for selling your car, listing mileage, colour, age, and price.
In the other, advertise for 'Flat sharing'.

figure 7

JU7	JU7	JU7	JU7	JU7	JU7	JU7	JU7	JU7	JU7	JU7	JU7
U7J	U7J	U7J	U7J	U7J	U7J	U7J	U7J	U7J	U7J	U7J	U7J

figure 8

KI8	KI8	KI8	KI8	KI8	KI8	KI8	KI8	KI8	KI8	KI8	KI8
I8K	I8K	I8K	I8K	I8K	I8K	I8K	I8K	I8K	I8K	I8K	I8K

figure 9

LO9	LO9	LO9	LO9	LO9	LO9	LO9	LO9	LO9	LO9	LO9	LO9
O9L	O9L	O9L	O9L	O9L	O9L	O9L	O9L	O9L	O9L	O9L	O9L

figure 0

;P0	;P0	;P0	;P0	;P0	;P0	;P0	;P0	;P0	;P0	;P0	;P0
P0;	P0;	P0;	P0;	P0;	P0;	P0;	P0;	P0;	P0;	P0;	P0;

Key the following sentences:

My lucky numbers are 3, 5, 7, 9, 24.

There were 8 children at the party.

He had to take 2 tablets 4 times a day.

Some people think the number 13 is unlucky.

Her birthdate was 3 August 1976 not 30 August 1986.

It took 4 weeks for the 2 men to complete the job.

He bought 6 lottery tickets.

Word Perfect 5.1 is a popular word processing package.

The booking is for 6 people.

The lecture room holds 70 people.

There were over 150 people at the conference.

102–105 Baggot Street, Dublin 2.

The company gives 30 days credit.

There are 15 company cars and 4 vans insured by us.

> —*Wrists Up*
> —*Fingers Curved*

> *Check Your Posture*

Display the following advertisement on A4 paper, centring both vertically and horizontally.

<u>THE INTERNATIONAL COMPUTER EXHIBITION</u>

Friday 26 October 19..

EXHIBITION CENTRE

DUBLIN 4

Opportunity to meet suppliers, watch demonstrations, use equipment.

Exhibitors will include:

* Leading Irish suppliers

* Leading International suppliers

* Industry related training and employment boards

* Professional institutions and associations

ADMISSION

Adults   £4.00
Students £2.00 (with ID)

For further information
and up-to-date details
call Frances or Gavin on
(01) 653215
or Fax (01) 653217

Display the following on A4 paper, centring both vertically and horizontally.

COMPUTER TRAINING CENTRE

Dublin, Cork, Limerick

<u>Specialists in all computer applications</u>

Following courses starting next month:

WORD PERFECT
DATABASE
PAGEMAKER
VENTURA
MICROSOFT WORD
DOS
WORD PERFECT FOR WINDOWS
WORD FOR WINDOWS
LOTUS 123

BOOK EARLY

<u>LIMITED SPACE AVAILABLE</u>

<u>EXCELLENT RATES</u>

For further details telephone

(01) 7690234
Fax (01) 7690237

Making corrections

With increased developments in technology, the "it's finished, it'll do" syndrome is long gone. Companies expect a very high standard from their workforce and it is vitally important that all your work is PROOF-READ for accuracy. If you have a spell-check facility on your machine, it should always be used - but not relied on to identify all mistakes. For example, the computer will not be able to differentiate between their, there, they're: it is the trained eye of the operator that notices these errors.

If you have found that your errors are excessive (more than four in the exercise on the previous page) then check your work.

— Are you keying character by character?
— Do you say each character to yourself as you hit it?
— Is your posture correct?
— Are you being over-ambitious by trying to key too quickly?
— Is your concentration poor?

All the above contribute to poor work and must be avoided. Get into the habit now of ALWAYS PROOF-READING YOUR WORK. At the end of each sentence check your work for errors and make any corrections necessary using the correcting facility on your typewriter or PC. In the next chapter we will introduce some manuscript signs that you are likely to encounter.

Take Note!

Exercise 4

	STROKES	WORDS
The Irish Association of Non-Smokers was founded in 1974	57	11
with the aim of establishing rights for non-smokers in	112	22
contemporary society. The Association seeks to promote	168	33
legislation restricting smoking in public areas and also	225	45
to create awareness of health risks from passive smoking.	282	56
Apiculture is the keeping of bees and there is an active	57	11
Beekeepers Association in Ireland. It aims to unite	110	22
beekeepers and foster efficient bee-keeping, honey	161	32
production and marketing. The Association has its own	216	43
publication called 'An Beachaire' (The Irish Beekeeper).	272	55
The Irish Wildbird Conservancy is the largest	46	9
environmental organisation in the country. It is	96	19
concerned with conservation, education and research in	151	30
relation to wild birds and their environment.	196	40

Display the following menu on A5 portrait, centring both vertically and horizontally, using the block centre method.

M E N U

Pate Maison
Melon in Port
Fruit Juice
Spring Rolls
Smoked Salmon

*****

Roast Duckling
Fillet Steak
Lemon Sole
Rack of Lamb

*****

Eclairs
Selection of Ice Cream
Fresh Fruit Salad

*****

Tea or Coffee

Block centre

o Find the longest line in the text.

o Centre this line, and set the left margin at this point.

o Type all the text at this margin.

Display the following on A5 landscape. Centre both horizontally and vertically using the block method.

THE TYRE CENTRE

All leading brands of new & remould tyres available
Five minute puncture repair
Exide batteries always in stock
Tracking & Balancing

Open 6 days

26 Ballyfermot Road, Dublin 10
Tel 6153402
Mobile (088) 588123

Spaced capitals

o Leave one space between letters and three spaces between words.

Manuscript technique

Before typing always read through the text to make sense of it. If there are some words that you cannot read, check with the author or look the word(s) up in a dictionary. If this is not possible and you are unable to decipher the characters, leave a gap in the text rather than typing rubbish. Manuscript signs and symbols can be seen on page 33.

Exercise 5

The Data Protection Act 1988 was passed to deal with privacy issues arising from the increasing amount of information kept on computer about individuals. In giving new rights to individuals, the Act also put new responsibilities on those who keep personal information on computers.

Exercise 6

A postage book is suitable only for small firms. You record the exact amount spent on postage of all items – letters, parcels, registered mail – and the total must balance with that withdrawn from petty cash. This system is considered impractical and too time consuming an exercise for large organisations.

Exercise 7

If you want to upgrade your professional image with sophisticated high-quality letters and documents, then our latest laser printer is the one you need.

Key the following advertisement on A5 portrait, centring both vertically and horizontally.

```
PLANNING A HOLIDAY?
LOOKING FOR LATE AVAILABILITY?


BROAD TRAVEL

THE AUSTRIAN SPECIALISTS

-REDUCED PRICES-


*Hotel
*Pension B&B
*Flight only


PHONE NOW!!!!!!!!!!

01 532567
```

Remember

To leave 3 clear lines you must return 4 times.

Vertical centring

Even space at top and bottom of the page. If using a computer you may have an automatic facility for this procedure.

o Count each line of text to be typed, including blank lines required.

o Subtract the answer from the total lines on the page.

o Divide by 2—this is the number of clear lines which must be left at the top of the page.

Key the following menu on A5 portrait, centring vertically and horizontally.

```
DONEGAL ARMS HOTEL

Lunch Menu

Fruit juice
Soup of the day
Pate & toast

*****

Roast Chicken
Fillet of Beef
Plaice
Lasagne
Salad Buffet

*****

Apple pie & cream
Strawberries & cream (when in season)
Ice cream

*****

Tea/Coffee
```

Change your line space indicator to 1.5. If working on a computer go into your format to change the line spacing.

Exercise 8

	STROKES	WORDS
The simplest definition of water pollution is "the loss	56	11
of any of the actual or potential beneficial uses of	109	21
water caused by any change in its composition due to	162	32
human activity". The beneficial uses of water are varied	219	44
and include its use for drinking and for domestic	280	56
purposes, for watering livestock and the irrigation of	334	67
crops, for fisheries – both game and coarse, for industry	392	79
and for food production, for bathing and for recreational	450	90
and amenity use.	467	94
If water is rendered unsuitable for any of these purposes	524	105
then it is polluted to a greater or lesser degree	574	115
depending on the extent of the damage caused. The	624	125
inclusion of the word 'human' in the definition is	675	135
necessary because water may be naturally impaired in	708	142
quality either temporarily or permanently.	750	152

(ENFO - Briefing Sheet 11)

The UNDERSCORE or UNDERLINE character is usually located on the same key as the hyphen and is used to give emphasis to text. You simply key the word as usual, use the backspace key to return to the beginning of the word, hold down the shift key and hit the underscore. If you are working on a computer or electronic typewriter you will have the facility of underlining as you key the text: refer to your user's manual/template. Do not underscore final punctuation marks.

eg

Please send <u>2 only</u> samples of each item.
The advertisement was for a <u>temporary</u> legal executive.
<u>Katie Harrington</u> and <u>Jim Bolger</u> have been nominated for the Presidency of the club.

<u>OPERATOR ASSISTED CALLS</u> cost more money.
Join our tele-sales team – <u>excellent rates</u> for experienced personnel.

Using A5 portrait, key the following exercises, centring each individual line.

Return 14 times before starting.

THINKING OF BUYING

A

NEW CAR?

LOOK NO FURTHER

SPECIAL DEALS

for month of June only

Volkswagen Polo
Mazda 121
Mazda 323
Ford Fiesta

EXCEPTIONAL VALUE FOR MONEY

COME IN AND SEE US ASAP

Horizontal centring

o Set the left margin at 0 and move the right margin stop to the extreme right.

o Set a tab stop at the mid-point of the paper:

eg (12 pitch) A5 portrait 35
A5 landscape 50

o Count the number of characters on a line, including spaces, and backspace half that amount. (If the figure is uneven, ignore the extra character.)

eg   FOR SALE
(8 characters, backspace 4 times)

Key the following advertisement on A5 portrait, centring each line.

Return 18 times before starting.

Check paper sizes on page 30.

Make sure you carriage return from the top edge of your paper.

GOLF CLUB MEMBERSHIP

EXCLUSIVE 18-HOLE GOLF COURSE

NOW OPEN FOR MEMBERSHIP

*Convenient Location
*Attractive Terms
*Limited membership

FOR FURTHER INFORMATION

Contact Mr L Nolan
061 567892

Underscore the titles in the timed exercises to follow.

Exercise 9

(ENFO – Briefing Sheet 17)

	STROKES	WORDS
The Dublin area is not associated with castles – perhaps	56	11
with 'the Castle' in the sense of it being the old seat of	115	23
administration – but not with the massive and spectacular	174	34
architectural tour de force that constitutes the popular	232	46
image. Castles were both homes and powerful machines	285	57
for attack and defence and it is not generally realised	341	68
that the Dublin area once possessed perhaps the highest	396	79
concentration of these in Ireland. Unfortunately for	449	89
our heritage the destruction rate in the past has been	503	100
appalling and is continuing. The castles that have	554	110
been suffered to survive give some impression of what	607	121
used to be – and what a superb impression this is,	657	131
since it includes architectural detailing and castle	709	141
unique to types which are this country.	748	149

Sitting up Straight?

Exercise 10

(ENFO – Briefing Sheet 20)

Dublin is a great city with a lengthy and rich history of	57	11
achievement. Over the centuries countless visitors have	114	22
written both of the splendour of its setting and the	167	33
magnificence of its architectural heritage. But like any	224	44
other great city, Dublin cannot be understood just in terms	284	56
of its buildings or its property, its streets or its squares. It is	345	69
much more – a centre of literary, cultural and artistic	400	80
achievement. Dublin is a vast collection of memories and	460	92
expressions of emotion with the greatest concentration	515	103
of meaning at its centre. Dublin is the national capital;	571	114
it is the symbol of Ireland as well as being home for	624	124
almost one third of the State's population.	667	133

Eyes on Copy

Exercise 11

(ENFO – Fact Sheet 15)

Trees are the largest living organisms in the world. Plants	60	12
and especially trees are primary producers. They produce	120	24
food in the leaves by photosynthesis, taking carbon dioxide	181	36
from the atmosphere, combining it with water and energy	241	48
of sunlight. This food which forms the beginning of the	300	60
food chain is essential for all other forms of life.	352	70
The mild and moist climate of Ireland favours the rapid	407	81
growth of trees. Trees in Ireland have good soil, a ready	462	92
supply of water and there are not extremes of temperature	519	103
to check their growth. Because of these factors trees	573	114
grow over three times faster in Ireland than they do	626	125
in mainland Europe. A newly planted sapling about	680	136
1m high may have trebled its height in five to six years.	738	147

Fingers on the Home keys

Centring

Text can be displayed both horizontally and vertically. In order to calculate position of typing you need to know your paper sizes, both length and width. If you are working on a computer then you will be able to centre automatically and change your paper size to match the task.

Make your display attractive to the eye with the use of underscores, upper and lower case characters, bold print and extra decorative symbols.

Change your line space indicator to 1.5 line spacing.

TREES FOR WILDLIFE

	STROKES	WORDS
Woodland offers a habitat or home for many of our native	57	11
species of plants and animals. It forms a rich habitat with	118	23
its ground layer of bluebells, violets and primroses and its	180	36
shrub layer and associated tree canopy. Trees provide birds	241	48
with food, cover, nest sites and song posts. Food is	295	59
available directly in the form of buds, seeds and fruit and	355	71
indirectly as a result of the insect life that plants support.	419	84
Some of our native trees such as oak, ash, birch and hawthorn	480	96
support numbers of insects which in turn are a source of food	541	108
for many species of birds, such as tree creepers, blue tits,	601	120
wrens and warblers. One in every two Irish insect species is	660	132
dependent on these woodlands for its home. Other birds	719	144
like the blackbird, the thrush and the wood pigeon eat the	778	155
berries and seeds of trees and shrubs during the winter when	839	169
other food is scarce.	862	172
Trees also offer shelter from harsh weather and cover for	920	184
nesting birds. An old decaying tree with a hole or cavity in	982	197
its trunk may become the home of an owl. Smaller holes may be	1045	209
used as nest sites by blue tits. Accumulated leaves on the	1101	220
woodland floor are ideal food for many species of insects	1159	232
which in turn are eaten by woodland birds.	1203	241
Well established woodland areas are also inhabited by mammals	1265	251
such as the fox, the red and grey squirrel and the red deer.	1326	265
The squirrel is the mammal most closely associated with trees.	1389	278
The red and grey squirrel are easily distinguished by colour.	1451	290
The red is distributed over most of the country but being	1509	302
shyer than the grey is not seen as often. The grey squirrel	1570	314
was introduced into this country and is found in only a	1626	325
smaller number of counties. Both species eat the seed of	1684	337
woodland trees.	1699	340

(ENFO – Fact Sheet 15)

FINDINGS (Contd)

3.4 We contacted four companies who have introduced uniforms in the past two years and they all stated their satisfaction at the results. Copies of these letters are attached. (Appendix 2)

3.5 Gray Mahon & Associates, our Image Consultants, stated that the concept of corporate identity is widely proclaimed as being re-assuring to customers. They feel that an attractive, well-cut uniform would enhance our image with the public.

4 CONCLUSION

The working party feel that the introduction of a uniform is a viable proposition and recommend that the idea be agreed in principle.

5 RECOMMENDATIONS

5.1 That the Board decide on the cost implications, possibly offering interest-free loans to employees to purchase the uniform

5.2 That if the Board decide to proceed with this project that an Action Committee be set-up comprising members of Personnel and Administration who will decide on design and implementation. A representative of Gray Mahon & Associates would be happy to serve on the committee in a consultative capacity.

Signed _____   Date _____

Keyboard revision

Key	Meaning	Spacing
?	Question mark	<u>two spaces</u> after at end of sentence
-	Dash	<u>one space</u> before and after
"	Quotation marks	<u>no space</u> within the quotation eg "The Sunday Review"
		<u>one space</u> before and after
( )	Brackets	<u>no space</u> before or after
-	Hyphen	<u>no space</u> before or after
'	Apostrophe	<u>no space</u> before or after
&	Ampersand	<u>no space</u> before or after
/	Oblique	<u>no space</u> before or after
@	At	<u>no space</u> before or after
%	Percentage	<u>no space</u> before <u>one space</u> after
£	Pound sign	<u>no space</u> after

This time change the line space indicator to 2 and compare the difference between that and 1.5.

THE GREENHOUSE EFFECT

	STROKES	WORDS
People use the Earth's resources to try to improve their	57	11
lives – that is development. They need to look after the	115	23
Earth to make sure it continues to provide the	162	33
resources – that is conservation. Finding the right	215	43
balance between development and conservation is a major	271	54
issue facing people today.	299	60
The growth of industrialized societies has brought huge	355	71
changes to the lives of people living in them, mainly for	414	83
the better, and the standard of living has improved. All	471	94
these changes have contributed to improvements in quality	530	106
of life.	540	108
These improvements have been made possible by progress in	598	120
science, which finds out about the forces of nature and	654	130
technology and which attempts to harness these forces.	706	141
Agriculture and industry have then applied this knowledge	763	153
to their activities. In doing this the environment is	818	164
changed and sometimes damaged. If the world is to be	872	174
productive and pleasant to live in, we need to know more	929	186
about how the world works and what effects our activities	987	198
are likely to have on the natural processes on which we	1043	209
depend for food, water and countless other resources	1097	219
essential for our survival.	1124	225

(ENFO – Fact Sheet 16)

Long Report

CONFIDENTIAL

FOR   P J Halpin, Managing Director   REF   HTD/00346B

FROM   H T Dickenson, Chairman,   DATE   14 February 19 - -
Working Party

REPORT ON THE PROPOSAL TO INTRODUCE A UNIFORM FOR STAFF

1   TERMS OF REFERENCE

On 7 January 19 - - the Managing Director instructed a specially set up working party to investigate the practicality of introducing a staff uniform for all departments and to make appropriate recommendations. The report was to be submitted to him by 21 February 19 - - for the consideration of the Board of Directors.

2   PROCEDURE

In order to obtain relevant information and opinion, the following procedures were adopted by the working party:

2.1   A questionnaire was distributed to all staff to canvass opinion.

2.2   The committee agreed to source potential suppliers.

2.3   The personnel department were asked to anticipate potential problems.

2.4   Several other companies who had introduced uniforms in the past eighteen months were contacted and their opinions sought.

3   FINDINGS

3.1   Over 75% of those canvassed agreed in principle to the introduction of a uniform. They sought clarification on the grades of personnel involved and the contribution, if any, the staff would be required to make.

3.2   While several designers stated they would be happy to submit designs the committee felt that it would be more appropriate to use a specialist in this area and attach to this report brochures with prices from two companies who have been highly recommended. (Appendix 1)

3.3   The personnel department asks that we consider the following questions

       3.3.1   Should male and female staff be required to wear a uniform?

       3.3.2   If a uniform is introduced, will it be compulsory for all staff?

       3.3.3   What about long-term temporary/contract staff?

       3.3.4   What about middle-management/managerial staff?

       3.3.5   Loss of identity?

       3.3.6   Younger staff members and the 'back to school' feeling?

       3.3.7   Exemptions for pregnant women?

       3.3.8   Classic rather than fashion cut to suit all shapes and sizes.

       3.3.9   Importance of involving staff in the choice of design.

Any of the timed pieces in this chapter can be used for copy practice or speed development.

HOUSEHOLD PLANTS

	STROKES	WORDS
The Yucca Plant has become a familiar sight in Irish houses in	62	12
recent years. Even so, we are still struck by its appearance, its	128	25
exuberant, arching leaves protruding from the top of a quite bare	193	39
stem. These Yuccas are usually produced by forcing imported stems,	260	52
or 'canes', to root and sprout in greenhouse conditions. This is	325	65
why they do not grow from the very tip of the canes (as they would	389	78
do if grown from seed), but to one side of the tip, giving the	449	90
plants an even more unusual look. The fact is that Yuccas grow	510	102
very slowly, so by producing what looks like a mature plant from a	574	115
cane, the growers are able to supply a hungry market quickly with a	639	128
product which, although still expensive, it is prepared to afford.	704	141
Yuccas come from South America. However, they are not hothouse	766	155
plants and are perfectly happy in a temperate climate. They	824	165
actually prefer to be left to rest in cool conditions (around 45°F	888	178
or 7°C) over winter which makes them the perfect plant for the	948	190
Irish householder. Yuccas can even stay outdoors for most of the	1012	202
year, and only need to be brought in when there is a danger of	1073	215
frost. The plant thrives best where there is plenty of light,	1134	227
including direct sunlight. During the summer months water	1191	238
regularly including a mild dose of plant food about once a month.	1255	250

Keyboard proficiency

The development of speed and accuracy is assisted by drilling commonly used words and phrases. The drills in this section should be keyed accurately, quickly and fluently. Always begin by keying within a controlled speed, with accuracy and good technique. From that sound base, increase your speed and fluency while maintaining accuracy. These drills are interspersed throughout the book.

Drill one line of each word.

DISPLAY,   DISPUTE,   DISMISS,   DISCUSS,   DISABLE,   DISMAY,   DISGUST
COMBINE,   COMPACT,   COMPOSE,   COMMEND,   COMPLETE,   COMPUTER

DEBATE,   DEDUCT,   DEPART,   DEPEND,   DEGREE,   DECIDE,   DETAIN,   DENY
ENABLE,   ENDURE,   ENACT,   ENCLOSE,   ENERGY,   ENORMOUS,   ENLIGHTEN

Informal report

FROM   J Bowman, Offices Services Supervisor

TO   T Roche, Purchasing Manager

DATE   3 March 19 - -

OFFICE EQUIPMENT

Introduction

The General Manager has asked that an investigation be carried out on the long term implications for the telex service from the introduction of high speed fax machines.   In particular he requests that the conclusions be made available to your department for the information of your staff. The following comparisons have been made of the two services.

Findings

T E L E X

ADVANTAGES

– All secretarial and clerical staff are familiar with the telex machine and its operation
– It is relatively inexpensive to operate as advantage can be taken of off-peak charges for transmission
– Over 90% of companies we have regular dealings with have telex machines installed

DISADVANTAGES

– To operate the system successfully the operator must have keyboarding skills
– The system is confined to transmitting alpha and numerical data

F A X

ADVANTAGES

– Each new generation of machine transmits at a higher speed
– As with telex this system can take advantage of reduced cost transmission if used during off-peak hours
– Keyboarding skills not necessary as the machine scans all data being processed
– The fax machine can transmit alpha, numerical and graphical data

DISADVANTAGES

– Not all of our contacts have introduced fax machines yet

Conclusions

It would appear that the trend is towards facsimile transmission and while telex machines will be in use for several years to come any future investments should be in fax machines.

Signed: ....

Key the following timed piece in 1.5 spacing.

<u>AQUACULTURE</u>

	STROKES	WORDS
Aquaculture is a key element in Bord Iascaigh Mhara's (BIM's)	62	12
strategy for the development of the seafood industry. Through	125	25
marketing, financial, technical and training support services, BIM	192	38
is actively promoting the development of Irish aquaculture in a way	260	52
that causes minimum environmental impact, while giving maximum	324	65
employment, income and exports.	357	71
It is making a major contribution to the economy in terms of	418	84
output, job creation and exports. This development has largely	482	97
been achieved within the space of the past ten years.	536	107
More importantly, the sector now provides employment for over 2000	603	120
people, mainly in remote coastal regions where there are few, if	668	134
any, alternative sources of employment.	709	142
While shellfish farming is generally regarded as having little	772	155
negative environmental impact, fin-fish farming has not been so	834	167
regarded. Several detailed studies have been undertaken regarding	899	180
the environmental impact of fin-fish farming. Dr Richard Gowen of	964	193
the Natural Environment Research Council in Britain, recently	1024	205
undertook a study on the environmental impact of waste from fish	1087	218
farms and concluded that there was no proof that fin-fish farming	1151	230
is a non-sustainable activity from an environmental point of view.	1216	243
This study was sponsored by the Department of the Marine.	1273	255
Salmonid farms, both existing units and new ventures, must comply	1337	267
with strict National and EC environmental regulations, the	1394	279
enforcement of which is being monitored by the Department of the	1457	291
Marine.	1466	293
BIM headquarters are located in Dun Laoghaire, Co Dublin and they	1530	306
will be happy to furnish you with any further details you require.	1596	320

Short informal report

REPORT

TO   Bill O'Brien, Human Resources Director

FROM   Brid McIntyre, Personnel Secretary

DATE   23 October 19 - -

CANTEEN QUEUES

<u>Introduction</u>

Many staff members have complained of excessively long queues and poor service from the canteen at lunch time.   This complaint has been supported by several department supervisors who report that staff are constantly late returning from lunch, some people by up to fifteen minutes.

<u>Findings</u>

There are three scheduled lunch times (a) 1200 – 1230, (b) 1230 – 1300, (c) 1300 – 1330. When the canteen supervisor, Deirdre Bowers, was interviewed she agreed that there was a problem. She feels, however, that her staff could cope if the lunch breaks were properly staggered.   At the moment employees go to the canteen when it suits them and most opt for the 1230 – 1300 time slot.

<u>Conclusions</u>

(a)   Each department should be allocated a specific time for lunch and asked to adhere to that.

(b)   A rota should be established to ensure that everyone gets an opportunity to have lunch at their preferred time.

(c)   A copy of this rota to be given to the canteen supervisor so that she can plan accordingly.

Signed _____

Revert to single line spacing for this exercise. Note the use of spaced capitals to enhance the display in the title.

When keying-in the title set the caps lock and leave one space between each character and three spaces between words.

H E L P I N G   D E V E L O P   Y O U R   M A R K E T S
– I N   I R E L A N D   A N D   W O R L D W I D E

	STROKES	WORDS
Bord Trachtala's activities concentrate on helping Irish companies	67	13
compete effectively in the Single European Market, within which the	135	27
vast bulk of Ireland's trade takes place. Beyond that horizon,	204	40
they also help to develop markets right across the world.	258	52
With the completion of the Single European Market, Irish companies	325	65
must now compete internationally on their home ground. More	386	77
sophisticated marketing and a greater strategic focus are now needed	456	91
than was the case before.	483	97
The rest of the Single European Market is a vast opportunity area for	553	111
Irish companies – but only if they can compete effectively. Ireland	622	124
now has to fight harder than ever to maintain its important share of	692	138
the UK market. Bord Trachtala's biggest priority as an organisation	761	152
is to help Irish companies integrate successfully in the post-1992	828	166
marketplace. One of their projects is to develop particularly close	897	179
relations with four key regions within Europe that are growing faster	967	193
than the rest.	983	197
Outside the Single European Market are important market opportunities	1053	211
for Ireland – some in traditional areas such as the United States,	1120	224
others in newer areas such as Japan. A network of trade consultants	1189	238
extends the reach of their office network in these world markets.	1256	251
How Bord Trachtala can help. Essentially, the organisation consists	1325	265
of a team of tightly-knit marketing professionals who help companies	1394	279
develop the right market for their product/services. They aim to	1457	291
help Irish companies achieve the competitive edge that is vital for	1522	304
success in the marketplace.	1551	310
You may access the services of Bord Trachtala in any of three ways –	1617	323
whichever is more convenient to you or suited to the particular need	1683	337
you have:	1694	339
– All services can be reached through your regional Bord	1756	351
Trachtala office, your convenient channel to all parts of the	1825	365
organisation.	1846	369
– You can also, if you prefer, directly contact head office	1911	382
services such as the specialist marketing advisors and the	1977	395
Market Information Centre.	2011	402
– For assistance in a particular market, you can contact	2076	415
the overseas office directly.	2107	420

Reports

Like memoranda, reports will vary in format, style, content and length, depending upon their purpose. They may be little more than short internal communications (like memoranda) between persons or departments, as for example in reporting on a minor departmental complaint. At the other end of the scale they could extend to very formal documents of hundreds of pages. It will be important, therefore, to distinguish clearly the sort of report required and prepare it accordingly.

Where it is of the shorter, more informal nature it will normally be broken down into three main component parts.

THE INTRODUCTION (background details, a description of the current situation, the reason for the report, and the means of assessment).

THE FINDINGS (information gathered on the subject).

THE CONCLUSIONS (including recommendations as to what action ought to be taken).

Note: It may be even less formal in that it may be presented in a memo form under the appropriate subject heading, with such sub-headings as are considered necessary.

Report writing style

Reports should always use impersonal constructions, eg 'It was evident' rather than 'I noticed' or 'I observed'. The absence of 'I', 'we' or 'my' lends objectivity to a report which should always confine itself to the facts and be devoid of any suggestion of bias, emotion or self-interest. Where it is necessary to supply opinion, as in the conclusions section, it should still be possible to produce these in an informed manner, free of subjective value judgements as far as possible.

Note the following examples. The first report is typical of a short, informal report prepared in-house by one individual. The second and third reports are longer and are more typical of the style of presentation used by a committee to present their findings.

Setting a tab stop

The function of the tab is to go straight to a pre-set point anywhere on the line and is particularly useful in exercises similar to the example here in that it saves you having to use the space bar to align the characters vertically. If using a computer either use default tabs or change settings in your format menu.

The first thing you do is clear existing tabs. Then count the number of characters and spaces in the vertical column on the left, add three spaces for display purposes and set the tab at that point. For example, in the following exercise 'Caoimhin (M)' has the longest number of characters at 12, add 3 for display, this total of 15 is added to the left margin of 12 giving you a total of 27 and this is where the tab is set.

Simply key the text in the left column, hit the tab key and you are taken immediately to the second column.

WHAT'S IN A NAME?

There has long been a tradition in this country to name children after their grandparents or close relatives. Even when this was not adhered to we were never very adventurous when choosing names, hence the plethora of Marys, Johns, Anns and Michaels.

However, in recent times there has been a growth in popularity in old Irish names. This is a list of some of the most popular along with some other unusual ones.

NAME	MEANING
Aisling (F)	'Dream' or 'vision'. Originally used in the regions of Derry and Omeath. Can be anglicised as Esther.
Cian (M)	'Ancient'. Old Irish name still in use today.
Conor (M)	'Hound lover'. An early Irish Christian name which gave rise to the surname O'Connor.
Darren (M)	'Little great one'. Has been very popular since the eighties.
Darerca (F)	Legend credits her as being the sister of St Patrick.
Gobnait (F)	Derivative of 'gob' – mouth. When not used in comedy sketches can be anglicised as Abigail.
Caoimhin (M)	Anglicised as Kevin. St Kevin founded the monastery at Glendalough. The feminine form of this name, Caoimhe, is currently very popular.

Keyboard proficiency

Drill one line of each of the following words:

VIABLE, USABLE, DURABLE, NOTABLE, MAILABLE, MOVABLE, SUITABLE
CHANCE, GLANCE, TRANCE, ENHANCE, BALANCE, FRAGRANCE

WENT, LENT, SPENT, REPENT, ACCENT, CLIENT, EXTENT, CONTENT
PAYMENT, COMMENT, MOMENT, SEGMENT, INCREMENT, GARMENT

5.1 Subscription Rate

The committee has completed a survey on membership rates and terms of membership in a variety of clubs, both in the district and outside, and suggests as follows:

Increase

Individual annual subscription	£500 (+£185)	
Family membership	£900 (+£300)	
Off peak times (9 am–4pm)	~~£250~~ (new category)	**75**
(Monday to Friday only)		

Group rates available on request

While the increases may seem high the committee feel that they can be justified in light of the increased facilities introduced in the past eighteen months. It should also be noted that there is a waiting list of approximately eight months. *↙ for membership*

5.2 Report on fund-raising activities

δ/

The ann~~u~~al 'Race Night' which took place on St Patrick's Night yielded a profit of £135 from the tote and brochure sales. In view of the amount of preparation and hard work involved it is seen as a very poor return and the committee recommends that some other form of fundraising be ~~thought of~~ *(considered)* for next year. The committee would welcome any suggestions *and will hold a brain-storming session at the next general meeting*

The Chairman thanked the Treasurer for his comprehensive report and asked that discussion on the Subscription rate be deferred to the September meeting when it was anticipated that there would be a greater attendance.

(6) Presentation on step-aerobics

Mr Alan O'Reilly of SPORTSWORLD introduced the concept of step-aerobics and stated that he would be willing to train our aerobics instructors.

→ The Chairman thanked Mr Alan O'Reilly for taking the time to come and give his presentation. Mr O'Reilly then left the meeting.

(7) Any other business

Prior to closing the meeting the Chairman asked that as many people as possible attend the July meeting as the question of fund-raising is v. important.

trs There being no further business the meeting closed at 9 pm.

(8) Date of next meeting

The next meeting will take place on Thursday 16 July.

Signed _____ Date _____

Type the following exercise as shown, proof-reading each section as you key it.

FORMS OF ADDRESS

To avoid embarrassment on both sides it is important that you always use the correct form of address. Not many people realise that the salutation frequently differs from the form of address on an envelope. We hope the following will be of assistance to you.

PRESIDENT

In speech as   A Uachtarain or, in English, President
In writing as   As above
Address on envelope   The name of the holder of the office comes first, followed by Uachtaran na hEireann or President of Ireland

TAOISEACH

In speech as   Taoiseach or A Thaoisigh
In writing as   Dear Taoiseach or Taoiseach
Address on envelope   Mr/Ms _____ TD, Taoiseach

MINISTER

In speech as   Minister
In writing as   Dear Minister
Address on envelope   Mr/Ms _____ TD, Minister for _____

AMBASSADOR

In speech as   Your Excellency or Ambassador
In writing as   Your Excellency or Dear Ambassador
Address on envelope   His/Her Excellency _____ Ambassador

BISHOP – ROMAN CATHOLIC

In speech as   My Lord or My Lord Bishop
In writing as   My Lord or Dear Bishop
Address on envelope   The Most Reverend _____ DD, Bishop of _____

BISHOP – CHURCH OF IRELAND

In speech as   My Lord or My Lord Bishop
In writing as   As above
Address on envelope   The Right Reverend _____ DD, Bishop of _____

CLERGYMAN – ROMAN CATHOLIC

In speech as   Father
In writing as   Dear Father
Address on envelope   Reverend _____ (CC, SJ etc)

CLERGYMAN – CHURCH OF IRELAND

In speech as   Mr
In writing as   Dear Mr
Address on envelope   The Reverend _____

Key the following Minutes following all manuscript changes.

KINSALE SPORTS & LEISURE CLUB

Minutes of committee meeting held on Wednesday 14 June at 7.30 pm in the Royal Marine Hotel.

PRESENT   Mr David Armstrong   (Chairman)
Mrs Hilda Begg   (Vice-Chairman)
Mr Richard McMahon   (Secretary)
Mr Gerald Browne   (Treasurer)
Ms Mary Conway
Mr Paul Daly
Mr Alan Fitzpatrick
Ms Geraldine Garvey

<u>In attendance</u>   Alan O'Reilly

(1)   <u>Apologies for Absence</u>

Apologies were received from Ms Michelle Lynch. *and Larry O'Toole*

(2)   <u>Minutes of last meeting</u>

The minutes of the last meeting held on 14 April were read, ~~approved~~ *agreed* and signed by the Chairman. *stet*

(3)   <u>Matters arising from the minutes</u>

There were no matters arising.

(4)   <u>Correspondence</u>

   4.1   A letter was received from the local Garda station advising that a number of residents *in Tudor Lawn* had complained about the noise after the last social evening.

        The Secretary was instructed to write to those concerned apologising for the inconvenience and stating that there would not be a further recurrence of this. *check spelling* It was further decided that a circular be written to all members asking them to take due care and consideration when leaving the premises.

   4.2   A letter was received from Active Sports, Patrick Street stating that there summer sale would begin on Monday next *19 June*. and that there would be great bargains. In addition, a discount of 10% would be given to members of Kinsale Sports & Leisure *Club* on production of a membership card. *The Secretary stated that he had placed a notice to this effect in reception.*

(5)   <u>Report from finance committee</u>

Mr Gerald Browne, Treasurer, presented the report of his committee.

Punctuation

OPEN and FULL punctuation

Open punctuation will be the style used throughout this book.

NB Open punctuation style does not alter the punctuation of continuous text; normal grammatical rules apply.

Open punctuation

When using this style of punctuation <u>no full stops</u> are inserted after initials or in abbreviations, a space is inserted instead.

eg   Mr J S Fitzpatrick
        Miller & Co

Full punctuation

When using this style of punctuation <u>full stops</u> are inserted after initials and in abbreviations.

eg   Mr. J. S. Fitzpatrick
        Miller & Co.

<u>Further Examples</u>

<u>Open</u>	<u>Full</u>
8.30 am	8.30 a.m.
1800 hrs (24 hr clock)	1800 hrs.
RSVP	R.S.V.P.
eg	e.g.
20 September 1994	20 September, 1994
PLC or plc	P.L.C. or p.l.c.

Revision exercise

Word division

Divide the following words adhering to the rules previously given:

MISDEED, FEELING, HERRING, SELF-TAUGHT, MELANCHOLIA, MENTION, WATERFORD, MARGIN, CHILDREN, 21,350, TELEPHONE, SUBSIDY, DISLIKE, ICOS, 13.05 am

Input the following documentation for the **KINSALE SPORTS & LEISURE CLUB.**

Key the following Notice and Agenda on A5 landscape.

KINSALE SPORTS & LEISURE CLUB

Meeting to be held in the Round Room, Royal Marine Hotel on Wednesday 14 June at 7.30 pm.

AGENDA

1   Apologies for absence

2   Minutes of last meeting

3   Matters arising

4   Correspondence

5   Report from Finance Committee

    (a) Recommendation on future subscription rate
    (b) Report on fund-raising activities

6   Presentation by Mr Alan O'Reilly, Sportsworld on step-aerobics.

7   Any other business

8   Date of next meeting

Richard McMahon
Secretary

Key the following Notice of a Meeting on A5 landscape.

KINSALE SPORTS & LEISURE CLUB

A meeting will be held in the Royal Marine Hotel on Wednesday next, June 14 at 7.30 pm. The agenda will be circulated later.

Richard McMahon
Secretary
Tel 021 543456

The majority of business documents are typed on A4 size paper with the following dimensions.

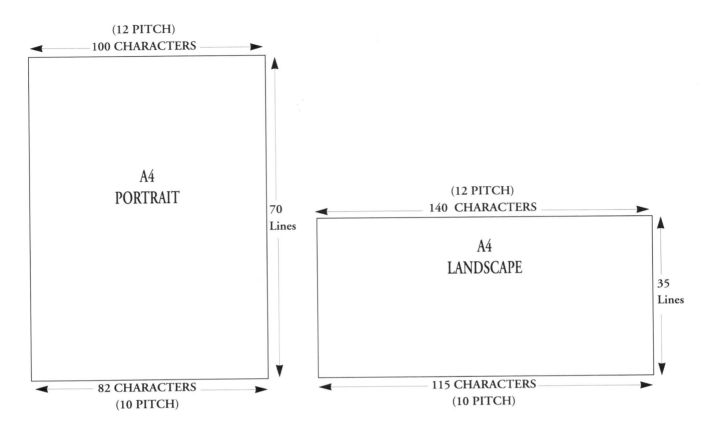

But some documents, eg short memos, short business letters and personal letters are typed on A5 paper which is half the size of A4.

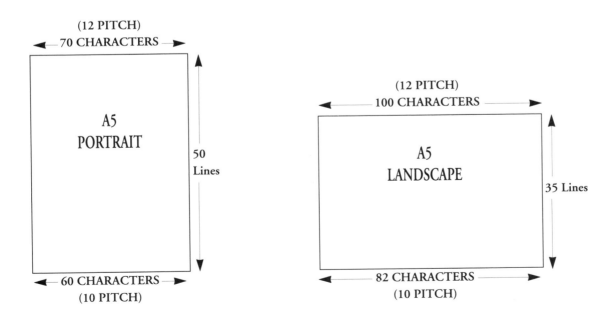

4   CHAIRMAN'S REPORT

The Chairman stated that he was pleased with the turnover to date and that sales were well up on last year's for this quarter. He attributed this to the success of the two new products which had been launched at the beginning of the year.

5   FINANCIAL CONTROLLER'S REPORT

The Financial Controller reported a 5% increase in profit on the same period last year. The budget was maintained well within the estimated figure. Expense accounts were kept on a level with last year. He stated that he would be happy to see this continue.

6   NEW PLANT

Mr Swan reported on development of the new Plant. The construction should be completed by early spring and to date spending was well within budget. He stated that all of the work on site, including landscaping, should be completed by the end of May. The Chairman thanked Mr Swan for his contribution to the meeting and complimented him on the progress to date.

7   OVERSEAS MARKETS

Ms A Wright reported on the development of the Spanish and Japanese markets. Spanish market on target with last year. After her recent trip to Japan, Ms Wright feels confident that the Company will secure a number of projects which will prove lucrative to the Company.

8   ANY OTHER BUSINESS

There was no other business.

9   DATE OF NEXT MEETING

The date of the next Board Meeting was fixed for 20 March 1994.

Signature . . . .   Date . . . .

Keyboard technique

Drill one line of each of the following:

CONTACT, CONFINE, CONTINUE, CONTRACT, CONCEPT, CONVOY, CONFUSE
MYSTERY, NURSERY, POTTERY, DRUDGERY, BRAVERY, FIERY, VERY

BRING, CLING, WRITING, CHOOSING, HEATING, SITTING, FILING,
POROUS, RAUCOUS, HIDEOUS, FAMOUS, CALLOUS, JEALOUS, CONTEMPTUOUS

Memos and Manuscripts

Memos are a quick form of communication between departments or branches of an organisation. Many companies have their own, pre-printed, forms but if these are not available the following formats are acceptable.

Short memos are typed in single line spacing on A5 landscape. Set margins of 1" on either side and a tab three spaces to the right of the longest character in the left column.

All the memos in this chapter use the BLOCK style of display.

M E M O R A N D U M

FROM   Facilities Manager
TO   Personnel Officer
DATE   3 April 19 - -

CANTEEN COMPLAINT

I have been advised by the Catering Supervisor in the Staff Canteen that some people are ignoring the 'No Smoking' signs. There have been numerous complaints as a result and I must ask you to take appropriate action to amend this situation.

M E M O R A N D U M

FROM   Marketing Director
TO   Tele Sales Staff
DATE   12 September
RE   Extra Bonus

In addition to usual commission payments all those who reach their monthly targeted sales will be given luncheon vouchers for the next three months.

— Always form complete sentences but minimise the content to basic points — sufficient to get the message across.

— M E M O R A N D U M typed in spaced capitals, ie with shift lock down and one space between each character.

— The subject heading is typed in closed capitals or with initial caps and the underscore.

— There is no salutation (Dear . . .) or complimentary close (Yours . . .) in a memo.

Minutes

The MINUTES of a meeting should be a brief, accurate and clear record of proceedings. Minutes are typed in the order in which items appear on the Agenda. They are typed in single line spacing, with double between points. Use either shoulder or side headings.

A description of the meeting, the time, date and place are given together with a list of those present. The minutes of the previous meeting are read by the committee Secretary at the start of each meeting and must be signed by the Chairman before the business in hand can begin. A space is provided, at the end of the Minutes, for the Chairman's signature.

Minutes are either typed on good quality bond paper and pasted to a minute book or typed on loose leaf minute paper and inserted into the minute book which comes in the form of a ring binder. As always, accuracy is extremely important with this document.

Type the following example on A4 with margins of 1" top and bottom, left and right.

Key the following Minutes all on one A4 page.

CITY ENGINEERING COMPANY LTD

Minutes of the Board Meeting held at Head Office on 14 March 1994 at 1400 hrs.

<u>Present</u>

Mr John McKenna	(Chairman)
Ms S Jones	(Secretary)
Mr J Hunter	(Treasurer)
Mr D Smithson	
Ms P Coady	

<u>In attendance</u>   Mr M Swan, Architect
                              Ms A Wright

1   APOLOGIES FOR ABSENCE

     The Secretary reported that Mr A Hill was unable to attend as he was away on business.

2   MINUTES OF LAST MEETING

     The Minutes of the last Meeting held on 12 February were read and signed by the Chairman.

3   MATTERS ARISING

     There were no matters arising from the minutes.

If the emboldening facility is available on your machine set it for MEMORANDUM, to differentiate between the main and sub-headings. You may also choose to set full justification to have an even right-hand margin. This can look particularly effective with a long document such as this.

MEMORANDUM

TO   All Department Secretaries/PAs

FROM   Bob Henderson, Security Officer

DATE   23 February 19 - -

SUBJECT   <u>Visitors to Head Office</u>

There have been several serious breaches in security in recent weeks and members of my staff have encountered strangers wandering throughout the plant unattended. Please be advised that the following procedures must be enacted and advise any new staff in your section accordingly.

o   Staff members must wear their identification badges at all times.

o   Instruct your visitor(s) to proceed on arrival to the main gate where security will direct them to a car parking space and give them a sticker for the car. Entry permits may be sent out in advance where an appointment has been made 2 – 3 days previously. <u>It is very important that security are notified of all expected visitors.</u>

o   They will then be directed to the main reception where they will be required to sign the Visitor's Book.

o   All visitors are issued with special 'Visitor' badges by Reception. Please ensure that this is worn for the duration of their visit and returned to reception prior to their departure.

o   If there are visitors to your department please ensure that they are accompanied by a member of staff on all occasions. If you must leave your office unattended for a few moments make sure that there is no confidential information on your desk and that all confidential documents on the computer are protected by a security password.

o   Do not discuss security details ie location of keys, storage of permits or access to software security, in front of visitors.

o   Be aware of the importance of security at all times.

Your co-operation in this matter would be appreciated.

We now move to manuscript work and while it is very important that you are familiar with the correction signs it is essential that you make sense of your work. Before keying the text always read through the item and check any words you are not familiar with. Have a dictionary to hand and proof-read the document before printing.

Key the following Notice and Agenda.

<u>CITY ENGINEERING COMPANY LTD</u>

A Board Meeting will be held in Head Office on 14 March 1994 at 1400 hrs.

AGENDA

1   Apologies for absence

2   Minutes of last meeting

3   Matters arising

4   Chairman's Quarterly Report

5   Treasurer's Quarterly Report

6   Plans for building of new Plant. Presentation by Mr M Swan, Architect

7   Developments for overseas markets. Ms A Wright to give report on progress and recent developments

8   Any other business

9   Date of next meeting

The Chairman's Agenda differs in that a space is left on the right side of the page for him/her to make notes. Set right margin to stop at 53 (12 pitch) or 45 (10 Pitch) and input the following example. Use margin release to type 'NOTES' heading.

AGENDA   <u>NOTES</u>

1   Apologies for absence

2   Minutes of last meeting

3   Matters arising

4   Chairman's Quarterly Report

5   Treasurer's Quarterly Report

6   Plans for building of new Plant
     Presentation by Mr M Swan, Architect

7   Developments for overseas markets
     Ms A Wright to give report on progress
     and recent developments

8   Any other business

9   Date of next meeting

Correction signs

Most of the documentation presented for input in the work situation is either hand-written or, more likely, printed with manuscript revisions. It is very important, therefore, that you are familiar with these printer's correction signs, their markings in text. what the instruction means and most of all how you correct it.

Text mark	*Proof mark*	*Meaning*	*Correction*
Annual	Sp Caps	Spaced caps	A N N U A L
Dear Mr Arnolds	ʅ	Delete	Dear Mr Arnold
Ex plain		close up	Explain
yesterday The main	ʌ⊙	insert full stop	yesterday. The main
william	uc	upper case	William
details of Text	lc	lower case	details of text
the train was going	#	insert space	the train was going
On [Monday	{/	move over space	On Monday
May June	ʌ,	insert comma	May, June
large box	stet	let it stand	large box
blue, pink	trs	transpose	pink, blue
company	caps	capitals	COMPANY
[When he took the	NP or //	new paragraph	
//The rain fell			
over watering	/–/	insert hyphen	over-watering
Do not	us	underscore	Do not
over recent			
years growth	run-on	run text together	over recent years growth
	ʌ:	insert colon	
	ʌ;	insert semi-colon	
	/ – /	insert dash	
	'	insert apostrophe	
	"/	insert quotation marks	

Even if there are no Manuscript Corrections in Your Text
YOU MUST ALWAYS PROOF-READ

Committee Work and Reports

At some stage everyone becomes involved with a committee, either through their work, leisure or even the local residents' association. It is useful, therefore, to be familiar with the documentation involved. In this chapter we will deal with

Notice of Meeting

Agenda

Minutes

The notice of meeting and agenda are usually combined using A5 landscape or A4 portrait paper depending on the length of the text involved. The notice is sent to all members and must include the name of the committee and should include the organisation or company name, the type of meeting, the date, time and venue of the meeting. The committee secretary sends the notice. Note the following examples.

Key the following Notice and Agenda on A5 landscape.

FCD SPORTS & SOCIAL CLUB

A meeting will be held on Friday 15 October 1993 at 8.00 pm in the Royal Tara Hotel.

AGENDA

1   Apologies for absence
2   Minutes of last meeting
3   Matters arising
4   Correspondence
5   Report from the Treasurer
6   Forthcoming events
7   Christmas party
8   Any other business
9   Date of next meeting

Emma Lyons
Secretary

Type the following manuscript memos on A5 landscape and correct as marked.

Exercise 1

MEMORANDUM

To   Production Manager
From   Sales Manager
Date   7 October 19XX

ORDER NO 1256/34BX   tRS

Copy of above order attached. // Please
proceed to manufacture these items at once
and report progress to me ~~every friday~~. We   *[TWICE WEEKLY]*
[SHALL BE] ~~hope to~~ exporting the goods on ~~12~~ November,   *[18]*
Sailing from ~~Larne~~. stet   *[Rosslare]*

Exercise 2

MEMORANDUM

lc   From   FInancail Controller   tRS

     To   All Members of staff

     Date   13 September 19—

     Re   New arrangements with
             ← An Post

                     18 September
                                              stet
From Monday next/ all outgoing mail will be collected at 4.30 pm ~~each day~~ by An post. // Please ensure that all post for despatch   uc
check   is recieved by mailroom staff no later than 3.30 pm in order to facilitate sorting and franking.
Spelling
↲   Urgent mail received after that time can be sent via private courier but, obviously due to high costs involved, we wish to keep   ↲
↲@   this to a minimum.

     Thanking you in advance for your co-operation.

TELEPHONE MESSAGE

Date .... Time .... To ....

WHILE YOU WERE OUT

Mr/Ms ....

of ....

Phone No. ....

	Telephoned	Please call him/her	
	Wants to see you	Will call again	
	Called to see you	Urgent message	

MESSAGE

....

....

....

....

....

....

Signed ....

Exercise 3

MEMORANDUM

TO   Sue Henley, Receptionist
FROM   David O'Brien, Personnel
DATE   20 March 19--

Induction Course — CAPS + U.C.
<u>Simon Bates</u> / <u>Kathy McGuire</u>

Two new members of staff from the Branch
Office will attend the above course in Head
in full Office on <u>Wed.</u> next 29 March.

Please arrange hotel accommodation and ~~have~~ *ask*
Λ to Oliver Λ collect them from the train on Tuesday
NP at 6.00 pm. [~~They~~ *Simon and Kathy* will make their own way
to the Office on Wednesday morning, so keep
this in mind when booking the hotel.
Thank you

Abbreviations always retained:

  am = **before noon**
  pm = **after noon**
 etc = **and others**
  eg = **for example**
  ie = **that is**
 NB = **note well**
 Mr = **Mister**
Mrs = **Mistress**

Compose a form with your personal details to fit on A5 landscape paper.
Include information such as: name, address, telephone, nationality, next of kin, occupation, education, etc.

Key the following form on A4 paper using double line spacing.

Claim no .... Insured ....

Policy no .... Renewal month .... Cover in order ....

Broker .... Ref .... Premium Paid ....

Claimant .... Age ....

Occupation .... Date of accident ....

Accident details ....

....

....

Details of injuries ....

....

Medical prognosis ....

....

Estimated General Damages ....

Outstanding Estimate ....

Handler ....

Supervisor ....

Future Diary Date ....

Date .... Signed ....

Letters

Business letters are typed on company headed paper. They are usually typed on A4 size paper or occasionally on A5. There are letterheads provided for use with letters at the back of the book or alternatively you could do your own letterhead especially if working on a computer.

Fully blocked style and open punctuation are used in this book. This means that all text begins at the left margin and punctuation is used only in the body of the letter.

o   Leave a top margin (after letterhead) of minimum 1 inch.

o   Margins left/right. Right margin shouldn't be greater than left.
    Use 18/87 (12 pitch) 15/79 (10 pitch)

o   Type reference—if there is one, leave one clear line space.

o   Type date, leave one clear line space.

o   Type name and address of person to whom letter is being sent, leave one clear line space.

o   Type Dear . . . . . , leave one clear line.

o   Type subject heading (if applicable), leave one clear line.

o   Type body of letter leaving one clear line between paragraphs.

o   The complimentary close is typed one clear line after the last paragraph.

o   The sender's name is typed leaving a minimum of 4 clear lines after the complimentary close.

o   Type the sender's designation (not always used) in capitals directly under his/her name.

There are some other additions to the business letter and these will be introduced to you at a later stage.

Display Work

Key the following form in double line spacing using A4 paper. Then complete the details on the form with fictitious information.

INTERNATIONAL LANGUAGE COLLEGE

SUMMER COURSES

Booking Form

SURNAME ....

FIRST NAME(S) ....

ADDRESS ....

TELEPHONE NO. .... DATE OF BIRTH ....

COURSE CODE .... LEVEL ....

ACCOMMODATION REQUIRED: FAMILY/HOTEL/FLAT*

HAVE YOU EVER BEEN TO IRELAND BEFORE? YES/NO*

IF YES, FOR HOW LONG ....

AMOUNT OF DEPOSIT ENCLOSED ....

DO YOU WISH TO SIT EXTERNAL EXAMINATIONS? YES/NO*

SPECIAL REQUIREMENTS ....

....

....

....

....

....

* Please delete as appropriate

Key the following letter on A4 paper in single line spacing. The numbers in brackets refer to the number of clear lines which should be left.

> **SUBJECT HEADING** used to draw the addressee's attention to the topic being presented. This may be typed in closed capitals or with initial capitals and the underscore.

XL INSURANCES

45-50 Shanard Avenue, Dublin 9

Tel 01 324567
Fax 01 324566

(6)
15 October 1994
(1)
Ms Joan Reilly
124 Caherdavin Lawn
Caherdavin
Limerick
(1)
Dear Madam
(1)
EMPLOYER'S LIABILITY CLAIM
(1)
As you are aware the above case is one for settlement in due course. There may be some contributory negligence on the part of the plaintiff and we may be able to negotiate a reduction on this front. However, we would intend to open negotiations.
(1)
We would be obliged for your confirmation that funds are available to meet this claim and a cheque will be issued by return once we advise settlement details.
(1)
As you are aware, the present estimate stands at IR£20,000 against this case.
(1)
Yours faithfully

(4/6)
B Ryan
CLAIMS HANDLER

Key the following form on A4 paper. Use double line spacing and margins 12 pitch (12/90), 10 pitch (10/72).

CLAIM FORM

CLAIM CODE ....

INSURED ....

PLAINTIFF ....

OCCUPATION .... AGE ....

WAGES .... NETT ....

MEDICALS ....

PLAINTIFF'S SOLICITOR ....

PLAINTIFF'S COUNSEL ....

OUR SOLICITOR ....

OUR COUNSEL ....

HIGH COURT PROCEEDINGS ....

PARTICULARS ....

....

....

DEFENCE .... LODGEMENT ....

PROOFS ....

LIST NO. ....

COMMENTS ....

....

Key the following business letter on A4 in single spacing. Use the letterhead provided.

JTG/ba

30 November 19 - -

Mrs Felicity Moore
Manager
International Banks
SOUTHAMPTON
S07 3FR

Dear Madam

RE P M NORMOYLE MACHINERY LTD

We have been given your bank as a referee to whom we might apply for a credit-worthiness reference. Mr Patrick Normoyle, Managing Director of the above company, states that the company has dealt with you over many years and is in a thoroughly reliable financial position.

The order placed with us is for a considerable quantity of spare parts – the total value is £25,000, payable within 30 days of delivery. Delivery is to be in three parts, £15,000 on 1 January, £5,000 on 1 March and £5,000 on 1 April next. Would you be able to confirm that P M Normoyle Machinery Ltd are likely to be in a position to meet such bills? As Mr Normoyle has been in business for many years and must have had other suppliers we wonder why he has changed to us, rather than his usual suppliers. We are only too ready to supply him, but since he offered your name as a referee we feel it is prudent to seek your confirmation of the company's reliability.

An early reply would be much appreciated.

Yours faithfully

J K Glennon
FINANCIAL DIRECTOR

Note: For an English postal address,
the town is typed in capitals.

POSTAL CODE: Last item in the address typed on a separate line. Leave one clear space between the two halves of the code. If this is not possible then type the code 2 to 6 spaces to the right of the last line.

Forms

Forms are typed in 2 or 1.5 spacing. The full stop is used, in continuous form, to give a line, or occasionally a full unbroken line is used. A paragraph of continuous text may be typed in single line spacing.

When typing a form a clear space must be left on either side of text and dots, eg

TO .... FROM .... DATE ....

For form completion, the characters must not touch the line, but should hover just above the dotted line. You will need to use the variable line spacer to adjust the typing line in order to obtain the effect.

All dotted lines must end at the same point giving a justified right margin.

Key the following telephone message form on A5 landscape paper.

TO	FROM ....
OF	TELEPHONE ....
DATE	TIME ....
MESSAGE ....
....
....
....
....
....
....
....
SIGNED ....
OPERATOR

To: Bill White; From: Susan O'Connor; Wellington; 326178; today's date; 12.30 pm; Message: Order despatched by courier. Regards. Operator: Sinead Walsh

Key the following letter on A4 paper in single line spacing. Correct the text as indicated by manuscript signs.

XL INSURANCES

45–50 Shanard Avenue, Dublin 9

Tel 01 324567
Fax 01 324566

2 September 1994

Mr J L Snow
'Mission House'
34-37 Main Street
Blackrock
Co Dublin

Dear Sir

EMPLOYERS LIABILITY CLAIM

We refer to your letter dated 20 August **and**

lc We enclose for your information, copy facsimile dated 14 August received from the Insurance Broker ~~concerned~~. **del**

stet You will note that the insured have now gone into liquidation. The ~~Insurance~~ Broker was to meet with the insured and get further information which was to be forwarded to us but we have not received this. We have today written to the **yet** Brokers threatening withdrawal of indemnity unless full co-operation is received. We shall advise you of the outcome in due course.

stet Will you please advise us of the ~~up-to-date~~ **current** position on this matter? Has Notice of Trial been served? You might let us have a copy of same. You might also advise whether a List No. has been obtained.

Yours faithfully

Robert Fitzpatrick

Enc

> **ENC/ENCS: This means there is an enclosure(s) with the letter. It is typed 3 clear lines after the sender's name.**

WORK EXPERIENCE

06 – 09 1990   <u>Print & Packaging Ltd, Mayor's Walk, Waterford</u>

My duties included taking telephone orders, making deliveries
and generally assisting the Print Manager. This was a summer job.

06 – 09 1991   <u>The Long Bar, Shankill, Co Dublin</u>

Barman. Serving drinks, mixing cocktails and handling cash.

INTERESTS

I like sports and am a member of various clubs. My
main sport is soccer which I play weekly. In the summer I enjoy
various water activities.

ACHIEVEMENTS

. Treasurer, Students' Union 1991

. School Prefect 1987 and 1988

. Captained soccer team for the last two seasons

REFEREES

Mr M Mathews
The Long Bar, Shankill, Co Dublin

Telephone: 2852239

Mr L Reilly, Principal
City Business College, Dublin 2

Telephone: 6612345

The advantage of using a CV for job searches is that you have complete control of the information it contains, unlike application forms where the company requests information which is specific to their organisation's needs.

In addition to listing your personal details and educational qualifications, you can emphasise any achievements which you feel support your application.

Try to abbreviate the text to a maximum of 2 pages, using the above example as a guideline. Be honest and do not make false claims. The display is very important and you must always check the document for errors. If such a vital document were to contain errors it would reflect very badly on the attitude you may bring to a job.

Key the following letter on A4 paper in single line spacing. Make corrections as indicated by manuscript signs.

XL INSURANCES

45–50 Shanard Avenue, Dublin 9

Tel 01 324567
Fax 01 324566

17 December 1994

Mr J Brown
56 Brook Road
Dublin 7

stet Dear ~~Sirs~~ Mr Brown

PUBLIC LIABILITY CLAIM

We acknowledge receipt of your first Notification dated 14 January and subsequent letter of 7 February.

We confirm having replied to Ryan & Smith, Solicitors in the usual manner.

We ~~have arranged~~ are arranging to attend the insured on other matters and will discuss this case with them at that time also. No doubt we will have to await particulars of negligence and other details before any real investigation can take place as it would appear the insured are unaware of the particulars relating to the accident

stet Yours ~~faithfully~~ sincerely

J B Manning

Curriculum vitae

The presentation of your Curriculum Vitae is extremely important. It is a prospective employer's first impression of you so great care must be taken with the presentation. It must be clear, concise and without error.

Suggested lay-out: Margins 12p (18/90), 10p (15/75). Type section headings (personal, education etc) so that they stand out. The use of Side Headings makes the CV clear to read.

Key the example shown, then try working on your own CV.

CURRICULUM VITAE

PERSONAL

Name	Paul Richardson
Address	25 Grange Park Avenue, Waterford
Telephone	(051) 87263
Date of Birth	15 August 1972
Nationality	Irish

EDUCATION

1985-1991   Grannagh Community School, Waterford

1991   LEAVING CERTIFICATE

French	Higher	B1
English	Higher	B2
Business Organisation	Higher	B2
Accounting	Higher	C2
Economics	Higher	C2
Irish	Lower	B3
Mathematics	Lower	C1

Third Level   City Business College, 2 Brook Lane, Dublin 2

1991-1993   BUSINESS STUDIES DIPLOMA

Year 1
- Economics
- Business Administration
- Business Accounting
- Information Processing
- French for Business
- Keyboarding

Year 2
- Business Law
- Information Processing
- Business Management
- French for Business
- Management Accounting

CONTINUATION SHEET: Begin typing on the fourth typing line from the top of the page and type the page number, date and addressee, leaving one clear line between each one. Return three times and continue with the text.

Key the following letter on A4 paper.

Our ref B10045C

23 February 1994

Mr & Mrs P O'Regan
11 Parkhill Drive
Balbriggan
Co Dublin

Dear Mr & Mrs O'Regan

RE <u>11 Parkhill Drive, Balbriggan, Co Dublin</u>

Thank you for your kind instructions to offer the above property for sale. We set out hereunder the details of our discussions:

1   The property to be offered for sale by Private Treaty.

2   The price to be quoted £59,500 to include carpets, curtains, blinds in kitchen and light fittings.

3   All offers to be submitted to you for your consideration.

4   The Title is Freehold.

5   The Solicitor having carriage of sale is Mr Stephen P Cunningham, 20 Lower Baggot Street, Dublin 2. We would be grateful if you would write to him and advise him that you have instructed us to act as agents in order that he may forward to us any information that we as agents should have. Also, could you please give him written authority to uplift your Title documents to facilitate the drawing up of a contract for the sale.

6   Viewing will be by appointment only and we will telephone in advance to arrange viewings. All viewers will be accompanied by a residential division staff member or myself.

Type numbers at the left margin and set a tab for the text. If using a word processor use the indent keys for more than one line of text.

Itinerary

An itinerary is a document containing the details of a journey or trip. It should include all the information which executives will require from the time they depart until their return to the office. A copy should always be kept in the office.

The document is typed in single spacing with the main details centred at the top of the page. Each day is listed separately and both the day and date are underlined. It is easier to read if the times are broken down and listed as side headings. Type the following on A4 making the changes shown.

ITINERARY
Trip of Miss Valerie McMahon to Madrid   *La*

6 – 8 June

<u>Tuesday 6 June</u>

1230 hrs	Meeting with ~~General~~ Manager to finalise details of the trip *Marketing*
1330 hrs	Company car from office to airport
1430 hrs	Check in Dublin airport for flight EI 156 to Madrid
1530 hrs	Depart Dublin
1905 hrs	Arrive Madrid. Taxi to Don Carlos Hotel, Plaza de Espana Tel (91) 5414236. Dinner in hotel

<u>Wednesday 7 June</u>

0730 hrs	Breakfast meeting with Snr Juan Jose Sese *and Snr Carlos Sanchez*
0830 hrs	Car collect to visit Lladro factory in Madrid
0930 hrs	Meeting with Snr Ramirez, Production Manager and Snr Sese. Remainder of day flexible around their schedule
1700 hrs (approx)	Return to hotel. Dinner with representatives of Lladro at their invitation

<u>Thursday 8 June</u>

1000 hrs	Visit to Madrid Academy of Art. Meet with Snr Enrico Fabio, Head of Ceramic Art Department, to discuss work experience programme involving his graduates.
1100 hrs	Tour of ceramics workshop. Interview students interested in participating in the programme
1300 hrs	Lunch
1430 hrs	Return to hotel. Afternoon free for shopping/sight-seeing
45 18~~00~~ hrs	Check in Madrid airport for flight EI ~~593~~ to Dublin *385*
1945 hrs	Depart Madrid
2115 hrs	Arrive Dublin. Company car will collect

2

23 February 1994

Mr & Mrs P O'Regan

7   "For Sale" signs will be erected at our expense.

8   Brochures have been prepared and we await photographs being developed at our expense.

9   Advertising will be kept to a minimum. We acknowledge receipt of £150 in respect of same. A detailed account of advertising spent will be sent to you on the negotiation of a satisfactory sale.

10   Our fees are at the rate of the agreed sale price plus VAT payable on closing of the sale.

We hope the foregoing is to your satisfaction and we look forward to producing a satisfactory sale as soon as possible.

Yours sincerely

R M Burns

Display Work

Key the following text making changes as indicated.

OPTICAL DISKS (Read Only Memory)

Mention CD discs and one thinks of the near perfect sound reproduction when played on a CD player. The technology of CD-ROM is fast developing as a main source of information retrieval for business. Almost every month refinements are being added. The advantage of the new CD disc is that storage capacity is far greater than magnetic disc. (Once data is stored on disc it is permanent.) A CD-ROM disk can store up to 600 MB on one disc, the equivalent of an entire dictionary or encyclopaedia.

Academics and research students are finding this technology of great benefit in speeding up their searches while sitting at a desk.

CD-ROM technology is already used in most libraries. Each database can store thousands of pages of information on any subject. CD-ROM discs are being used to archive all kinds of business and scientific material. An increasing number of publications are being made available in this format.

Piracy is a very big problem in the software world. Companies loose billions of pounds. One solution seems to be shaping up in the format of the CD-ROM disc. Software would be given to purchasers in the form of the CD-ROM disc which is immune to copying.

VIDEO CONFERENCE

Today's technological revolution has meant that vast distances do not have to hinder work. It may not be feasible for 10 people to fly from one destination to another for discussion, a possible solution to this problem is 'Video Conference'. This allows Business men, Doctors, to confer and discuss using a video conference studio which is connected up via satellite with studios around the world. [Telecom Eireann operate three such studios — Dublin, Cork and Limerick. (and)

71

Proof-read the following letter and re-type making the corrections shown.

Ref AZ/10004

20 October 1994

Mr Colin McGuire
∧ Buyer   ∧ Senior
The Hardware Store
Ballina
CO MAYO

Dear Mr McGuire

We write in reply to the points raised during our meeting at your office on Friday last.

1 Tolerance on level of the tiles, is covered in the attached technical description.

5 2 We confirm that the slate supplied will not exceed 1̸0 mm in thickness nor will it be less than 7̸ mm in 8
thickness.

        dark grey
3 We confirm ~~black~~ grout will not stain the tiles, provided it is removed before it has cured and provided
the cleaning process in the removal of surplus grouting is done with normal care and attention.

4 Skirting will be supplied split.

                                                       Eoin
5 We have again been in contact with Divernsay Ltd. The man we have to contact, Mr ~~Jimmy~~ Marks, has
not been available but we have been given an assurance that he will contact your office very soon. We will
continue to try to pin him down.

                                  with technical data
6 We enclose revised laying instructions∧

7 The use of 'Flux' detergent does not have any detrimental effect on ~~Lionheart~~ Terracotta but we do   stet
recommend that the tiles are suitably rinsed after use of any detergent.

8 The sealer may be applied as the tiles are dry. This will depend on local conditions.

9 The specifications on our riven slate are being sent with this letter.

10 The maximum and minimum size of the tiles will be found on the attached technical data.

Another means of highlighting text is to choose very wide margins and where sub-sections or emphasis points are involved to use various means of making them stand out:

(a)   frequently used for sub-sections
i   as in the character i
-      the hyphen symbol
o   and the character o (sometimes filled in with black pen)

See how some are used to good effect in this exercise.

ENGLISH/FRENCH
Interpreters/Translators

Our client, an international group of companies with offices in all the major European cities, has vacancies for suitably qualified personnel for the above positions.

The range of duties will include

o   Two-way translation
o   West European market research
o   Bi-lingual telephone communication with France and Belgium

Candidates will be expected to have

i   Fluency in French
ii   A relevant third level qualification
iii Ability to produce their own typewritten text either on WP or typewriters.

The successful candidates will work as part of a team. Excellent remuneration for those looking for the right career opportunity.

Send CV to

        International Recruiters Ltd
        Enterprise House
        Lr Mount Street
        Dublin 2

        Telephone 6734983

Display the following advertisement.

International Business Exhibition. See the latest extensive Range of products. Simmonscourt RDS. 6-10 October 19-- Opening hours Tuesday to Friday 11 am to 9 pm. Saturday 9 am to 6 pm. Trade Free. Public Admission £3 Students - 3rd level only (on production of ID card) Details from: International Exhibitions, 4 Mount St, Dublin 2: 6794144   Fax 6794142

2

20 October 1994

Mr Colin McGuire

11 No chipping or flaking of sufficient severity to impair either the strength or the appearance of ~~Bluelamp~~ *Lionheart* Terracotta should be expected.

in full 12 Delivery of <u>approx</u> 60 linear metres of black coving would normally be within ~~three~~ weeks of *two* confirmation of order.

13 We have been in contact with our Insurance Company concerning a warranty for the product. We ourselves have every confidence in Lionheart Terracotta and we have had no experience of any structural problems such as decomposition through stress or wear. Doubtless an insurance bond can be arranged, but if this were to be done it would have to be reflected in the price charged. ~~We, as a company, stand up to the work load required of them.~~ We would replace any tile or section of tiling where it could be shown that the composition, manufacture or content of the tile was shown to be deficient. The tiles are guaranteed against thermal shock, and are guaranteed to conform to the technical character described in the accompanying treaties.

14 We will offer an inspection service during the fixing stage to the extent that we will ensure that the tiles are bring laid in an acceptable manner and that the ~~tile fixer(s)~~ is competent. *tiler*

15 In regards to the use of Lionheart Terracotta at the garage on the Naas Dual Carriageway we hope to be in a position to advise you on this site tomorrow.

We trust the above summarises the points of our meeting. If you have any further ~~points~~ *queries* please contact me as soon as possible.

Your sincerely
TILE WORLD INTERNATIONAL LTD

A J PATTERSON
Technical Adviser

Enc

> **THE COMPANY NAME is typed in capitals** directly under the complimentary close.

Another means of enhancing display is to divide the text into 2 columns. Simply set the margins to type the text in the left column first and then leaving a minimum of 5 spaces between the 2, set your second column. If using a computer use the column facility available on most software packages, remembering to turn the columns off when you wish to use the full width of the page.

LICENCE REQUIREMENTS FOR AQUACULTURE
<u>Republic of Ireland</u>

SHELLFISH FARMS

Shellfish farmers require

(a) <u>Sea Sites</u>

   –   An Aquaculture or Fish Culture Licence
   –   A Foreshore Licence

(b) <u>Land based pumped re-circulatory systems</u> (ie hatcheries and purification plants)

   –   A Fish Culture Licence
   –   Foreshore Licence (in cases where the installation utilises the State's foreshore)
   –   Planning Permission
   –   An Effluent Discharge Licence

FIN-FISH FARMS

Promoters of fish farming projects require different types of licences depending on the type and location of the proposed project.

(a) <u>Freshwater Site</u> (ie hatcheries)

   –   A Fish Culture Licence
   –   Planning Permission
   –   An Effluent Discharge Licence

(b) <u>Sea Sites</u> (ie fish pens)

   –   An Aquaculture or Fish Culture Licence
   –   A Foreshore licence

(c) <u>Land Based Sea Farms</u> (ie pumped sea water sites)

   –   A Fish Culture Licence
   –   A Foreshore Licence (in cases where the installation utilises the State's foreshore)
   –   Planning Permission
   –   An Effluent Discharge Licence

To apply for a licence the first step is to contact the <u>Aquaculture Section of the Department of the Marine</u>. Staff there will supply the necessary application forms and will advise on any particular requirements. The following information must be provided by applicants.

(a) An outline of the site on a 6" Ordnance Survey Map
(b) The required area in hectares
(c) The species to be farmed
(d) The farming methods to be used
(e) Experience (if any) of the Applicant in Fish Farming
(f) Name and address of the person or company applying
(g) Kinds of structure to be used and their proposed location within the area outlined
(h) Environmental Impact Statements (Fin-fish Sites where production is envisaged to be over 100 tonnes per annum)
(i) Additional technical and environmental data may be required by the Department even if a full EIS is not necessary.

Applications have to be advertised in local newspapers to allow submissions by interested parties to the Department of the Marine.

69

Key the following letter on A4 letterhead in single spacing using suitable margins.

Ref WZ/am/A2.1

Date

Director of Studies
Lansdowne Secretarial Institute
103 Melbourne Road
Bishopstown
Cork

Dear Sir/Madam

RE LEAH FALLON

The above named has applied to us for the position of
Receptionist in our Ashford office.

You have been listed as a referee on Leah's Curriculum
Vitae and I would be grateful if you would complete the
enclosed form and return it to me as soon as possible.
A stamped addressed envelope is enclosed for your
convenience.

Many thanks for your help.

Yours faithfully

(name)
. . . .
Recruitment Officer

Enc

Forms

**Forms are typed in 1.5 or double line
spacing.
The full stop is used in continuous form
for dots . . . .
One space is left before text and one space
after eg . . . . NAME . . . . .**

(See chapter 5 for more details.)

**Please key the attachment on A5 paper using
suitable margins.**

NAME OF APPLICANT . . . .

POSITION APPLIED FOR . . . .

LOCATION . . . .

NAME OF REFEREE . . . .

POSITION . . . .

Can you please comment on the following in relation to this
applicant:

PUNCTUALITY . . . .

ATTENDANCE . . . .

APPEARANCE . . . .

RELATIONSHIP WITH PEER GROUP . . . .

OTHER COMMENTS . . . .

. . . .

Thank you for taking the time to complete this form. The
information you have given us will be kept in our confidential
personnel records and will not be released to the candidate.

Use A4 paper, margins (12 pitch) 18/87 or (10 pitch) 15/72 for these <u>side headings</u>. Single line spacing with double between paragraphs. Begin the text 5 spaces after the longest heading. Your finished copy will have different line endings to the text on this page.

CPU	Central Processing Unit. Part of the hardware inside which the 'brain' of the computer is housed.
VDU	Visual Display Unit. This is the term used to describe the screen or monitor.
HARDWARE	All the physical parts of a computer. The screen (VDU), CPU, keyboard, printer.
SOFTWARE	This is the term used to describe the program of a computer or the package which the computer uses, as opposed to the hardware.
QWERTY	Standard English keyboard. Named from the first 6 characters of the top row of the keyboard.
FORMAT	The process which the computer carries out in preparing floppy disks for storage of data.
DEFAULT	Automatic settings or values in a program eg particular line spacing, margins etc.
WYSIWYG	What You See Is What You Get.
INDEX	Also known as directory or list. List of documents/files on disk.
CURSOR	A stationary or flashing signal often in the shape of a triangle or small dash to indicate where you are in the text.

Keyboard proficiency

Drill one line of each of the following:

LEGIBLE, TANGIBLE, VISIBLE, PLAUSIBLE
MENTION, SECTION, PORTION, NATION, RATION

UNABLE, UNUSUAL, UNWISE, UNSURE, UNDONE
ASSIST, RESIST, CONSIST, RACIST, ARTIST

CHAIR, ARCH, WHICH, SUCH, VOUCHER
PAGE, WAGE, POSTAGE, OUTRAGE, SHORTAGES

Key the following paragraphs using <u>paragraph headings</u>. Use A4 paper, margins 12p (18,87), 10p (15,72). Single line spacing with double between paragraphs.

<u>ROM</u> Read Only Memory. This type of memory is built into the computer and cannot be changed as it holds instructions necessary for operation. Information in this memory is not lost when the machine is switched off.

<u>RAM</u> Random Access Memory. This type of memory is programmed by the user each time the machine is switched on. Not a permanent memory, therefore data will be lost if it has not been saved before switching off.

<u>JUSTIFY</u> To produce a straight right-hand margin. Each character ending at exactly the same point.

<u>FIXED DISK</u> A disk inside the computer which is used for storing computer programs and text.

<u>FLOPPY DISK</u> A disk which is inserted into the disk drive for the purpose of storing data. These disks can vary in size; the most common sizes used nowadays are 3.5" and 5 1/4".

Circular letters

These are letters of the same content which are sent to a number of people.

The date may be typed:
  (1) 12 February 1993
  (2) February 1993 (month and year)
  (3) Date as postmark (these words are typed instead of a date)

Name and address of addressee: Not always typed, space may be left for insertion at a later stage. After the date leave approximately 9 clear lines then continue as usual. If no space is required for the name and address then simply turn up 2 single spaces after the date and continue.

Tear-off slip: Use continuous hyphens from edge to edge. After the complimentary close leave a minimum of 4 clear spaces, type the line, turn up 2 single spaces and type.

Key the following circular letter with cut-off reply strip. Date for today and leave spaces for insertion of the addressee details at a later stage.

Dear Sir/Madam

We have pleasure in sending you our new catalogue, which includes particulars of all our products.

May I draw your attention to the wide range of computer accessories available. Our disk storage boxes are in attractive opaque grey or brown and come in 5 1/4" or 3 1/2" sizes. We have a vast selection of anti-glare screen covers and copy holders. Virtually everything to make the operator's life easier is available through these pages.

When you have read through our catalogue I am sure you will find a number of items of interest. If you require any further details please telephone .... at .... A price list is also enclosed for your perusal.

Yours faithfully

GENERAL MANAGER

Enc

Please send me product literature on

ITEM .... CATALOGUE NUMBER ....

FROM .... POSITION ....

COMPANY .... TELEPHONE .... EXT ....

ADDRESS ....

....

....

Headings

One means of enhancing display is by the correct choice of headings. The standard headings you will encounter are PARAGRAPH, SHOULDER and SIDE HEADINGS. All of these can be typed in capitals, using initial capitals, with the underscore, or capitals and the underscore, depending on the text and number (if any) of sub-sections involved.

<u>PARAGRAPH HEADING</u>   Both the heading and paragraph are typed on the same line. Leave two spaces after the heading before typing the paragraph text.

<u>SHOULDER HEADING</u>

Leave one clear line after typing the heading and type the paragraph fully blocked.

<u>SIDE HEADING</u>   The heading is typed at the left margin. The text is typed at a tab stop across the page, usually 3 to 5 spaces after the longest heading. All text is aligned at this point.

Key the following exercises using the three types of heading given:

The following paragraphs have Shoulder headings. Use A4 paper, margins 12p (18,87), 10p (15,72). Single line spacing with double between paragraphs.

<u>ERGONOMICS</u>

Ergonomics is defined as the study of fitting the job to the person and is concerned with the overall working conditions of employees. The study encompasses systems furniture, facilities, decor and health and safety.

<u>SECURITY</u>

With regard to computers 'Security' has two meanings. Firstly where disks must be kept in safe conditions, away from fire, heat and water or any other risks. Secondly disks with confidential information must also be stored so as not to get into the wrong hands.

<u>NOTEBOOK PC</u>

So called because of its size, roughly that of a thick A4 notepad. They are designed for the traveller, to fit into brief cases. The age of the portable PC is here. Airlines are generally happy for PCs to be used on board, and X-ray machines shouldn't damage computers or disks, but don't take them through or near magnetic metal detectors.

This letter has been typed by a junior and contains a number of errors. Please proof-read carefully paying particular attention to spacing after punctuation. Also please amend as instructed.

Ref AZ/10004

21 July 1994

Mr Colin McGuire

/Senior Buyer

The Hardward Store

Ballina

CO MAYO

Dear Mr McGuire

We acknowledge receipt of your letter dated July 19, together with the copy of the letter from your client.

In response we advise as follows

1 Turpentine,(not turps substitute) enters the pore of the tiles more easily than linseed oil. The surplus *ls* evaporates and an oil residue is left.According to the ~~factory~~ *manufacturer* this serves to nourish and seal the inner pores of the tile. Turps is one of the main ingredients of teak oil.It is a derivative of sap of a pine tree and, ~~like linseed~~ *stet* *stet* ~~oil~~, has been the basis of most paint until quite recently. *ls*

2 We cannot be precise as to volume of either turps or linseed oil to be used. However we only seel turps in 5 ltr quantities and certainly, this would be more than sufficient for 17 yd² of terracotta.

bottles

3 Again, with linseed oil, we only supply it in 5 ltr containers, although we propose soon to supply 1 ltr ~~cans~~. *be* It is, as we have explained, difficult to ~~the~~ precise as to requirements and we would agree that ~~five~~ ltrs be *numeral* much more than required for a 17 yd² job.

4. White spirit is usually adequate for removal of surplus linseed oil which has oxidised on the surface. If this is not successful, then we would recommend the use of Xylene. This should be worked over the surface with a brush and then removed with a cloth. We can supply this product at £3.80 per ltr, plus VAT.

5 Acidulated water is used to remove mineral salt boom. Often vinegar is sufficiently strong. In more stubborn cases a proprietary remover such as HG Extra should be used. *Run on*

There has been some confusion here because when your client telephoned, from what was understood from the conversation, the problem seemed to be one of mineral salt stain.

NOTE TO TYPIST: Indent numbered text 3 spaces from left margin and change 'TURPS' to 'TURPENTINE' throughout.

Display Work

The objective of good display is to make the item visually attractive to the eye and easy for the target audience to read.

There are many ways of enhancing the display of your work through selective use of CAPITAL LETTERS, S P A C E D C A P I T A L S, underscored text, the **emboldening** facility, all of which are available on the most basic of electric typewriters (if you do not have the bold facility on your typewriter simply overtype three or four times to darken the impression).

Simplicity and consistency are the keys to success. Having decided on your style of display, be consistent throughout the text.

In the following exercise you will see how the use of side headings also helps to make the details easier to read.

JOB DESCRIPTION

Title	Purchasing Officer
Department	Purchasing
Location	Head Office, Shannon Industrial Estate
Responsible to	Purchasing Manager
Job summary	Ensuring the supply and delivery of specified goods at the best terms available
Essential education	Membership of the Institute of Purchasing and Materials Management, Certificate or Diploma holder or a minimum of 3 years buying experience in the industry
Hours of work	8.30 am - 5.00 pm Mon - Fri (overtime when pressure of work dictates)

DUTIES AND RESPONSIBILITIES

. ongoing research of the market for new suppliers/better terms

. negotiating terms

. placing contracts

. maintaining adequate records

. liaising with shipping and production departments to ensure delivery of goods at required times

2

July 1994

Mr Colin McGuire

~~From~~ having read your client's letter it seems clear to us that the problem derives from use of too much boiled linseed oil. too liberal an application of this product is a common error among people not familiar with it's use. It has to be applied sparingly, layer by layer, with ample time (minimum 24 hours) between each application. When the final layer has had ~~ample~~ sufficient time to try, a light coat of beeswax should be applied. Beeswax should also be applied very sparingly, and apatina allowed to develop over a period of time. When comes to maintenance, detergents should be kept away from the floor. Messes should be wiped ~~up~~ with a cloth. Of the wax finish has been marred, that area should be rubbed over with a little beeswax and then buffed.

We hope the preceding information will ~~allow your client~~ ~~enable you~~ to resolve the problem. Otherwise we would ask you to inspect the floor and give us your opinion. ~~as to the cause of the problem.~~ stet

A copy of this letter is being sent direct to your client.

Yours sincerely
TILE WORLD RNATIONAL LTD

A J Patterson
Technical Adviser

cc Mrs R O'Brien, 'The Thatch', Westport, Co Mayo

**Use letterheads provided
at the back of the book.**

1 Bealtaine 1993

C P Nic Niallais
81 Gairdíní na Scéimhe
Luimneach

A Chara

Go raibh maith agat as uacht do fhiosrú maidir lenár
gcatalóg tinteáin. Istigh le seo gheobhaidh tú ár
luachliosta.

Beidh áthas orainn dioltoír a chuir chugat le
meastáchan ar fhesitiú do tinteán nua.

Má tá eolas breise ag teastail uait cuir gloach
chugainn aon uair.

Mise le meas

Sean Ó Ceallacháin

1 Marta 1993

E P Ni Allúráin
76 Bothar Nangor
Baile Átha Cliath 4

A Chara

Ba mhaith linn cuireadh a thabhairt duit fhéin nó do
aon bhall do d'fhoireann chuig 'Lá Oscailte' a bheidh
ar siúl in Óstan an Túir ar an 15 Márta 1993.

Beidh taispeantas iomlán de ríomhairí gléasanna fax
agus clóscríobháin ar fáil. Fhreisin beidh tae agus caife
á riaradh i rith an lae.

Ag súil go mbeidh tú i láthair.

Mise le meas

Padhraic Ó Conaire

o   This letter is keyed on A4 with margins of 1" on either side.

o   A letterhead is used, therefore you should leave a minimum of 1" free before starting the letter.

OCEAN SAILING CLUB
Dun Laoghaire, Co Dublin

Telephone 280 5634

3 October 1994

Mr Miles Oakley
"Minerva"
Ashford
CO WICKLOW

Dear Mr Oakley

With reference to your letter of 20 September I attach a membership form for completion.

Your name has been mentioned to me by several members who have stated that they would be happy to nominate you. Can you arrange to have two current members propose and second you and return the form to me as soon as possible.

I will then put your application to the next committee meeting and if everything is in order I will be happy to welcome you as a member after that date.

Yours sincerely

STEPHEN CROWLEY
Secretary

APPLICATION FORM

NAME ....

ADDRESS ....

TELEPHONE (o) .... (h) ....

AGE .... LEVEL OF FITNESS ....

PREVIOUS SAILING EXPERIENCE ....

....

PROPOSED BY .... SECONDED BY ....

COMLETH INTERNATIONAL PLC

Comleth House, North Avenue, London SW1Y 2AR
Tel 01 789 0261   Telex Comleth 7899831

2 Mayo 1994

Sr. Vicente Ramos
Apartado 4673
Las Palmas de Gran Canaria

Estimado Sr. Ramos:

Lamentamos el retraso en la entrega de las mercancías corrrespondientes a su grato pedido del 4 de enero último, y comprendemos perfectamente el contratiempo que ha debido suponer con vistas a la campaña de invierno-primavera.

Nos hemos puesto en contacto con la agencia de transportes 'Fontana e Hijos' para averiguar las posibles causas del retraso, independientemente de las reclamaciones que decidamos presentar. Adjuntamos la carta que enviamos a dichos senores.

En lo sucesivo, y con el fin de evitar contrariedades de este tipo, les agradeceremos que nos formulen sus pedidos a primeros de diciembre, para que podamos servirlos antes de las fechas navideñas, y evitar retrasos como el de ahora. Las fechas de los vencimientos podrán seguir siendo: marzo, abril y mayo.

Les tendremos al corriente de cualquier noticia.

Muy atentamente

Jorge Somoza
Jefe de Ventas

Using the letterhead supplied key on A4 in single spacing. Set a tab for the description of the various areas.

Units of measures
The apostrophe is used for feet (') and the quotation mark for inches (").

23 July 1995

Mr T P Harris
The Birches
Shanganagh Road
CO DUBLIN

Dear Mr Harris

RE WILLOWBANK, SWORDS, CO DUBLIN

With reference to your telephone conversation this morning I wish to confirm that the above property is available at an asking price of £64,500. The details you requested are as follows:

ACCOMMODATION

GROUND FLOOR

ENTRANCE HALL   Cloaks closet, 'phone point.

LOUNGE/DINING ROOM   Attractive marble fireplace. Door to kitchen.
26' 2" x 11' 1"

KITCHEN/BREAKFAST ROOM   The dining area is fully carpeted and the kitchen has been fully re-fitted with most
15' 2" x 10' 0"   attractive oak units. The kitchen is plumbed for dishwasher and washing machine.

UPSTAIRS

REAR BEDROOM 1   Has an en-suite shower room and fitted wardrobes.
15' 10" x 11' 3"

REAR BEDROOM 2   Fitted wardrobes. Piped for TV.
14' 9" x 8' 8"

FRONT BEDROOM 3   Fitted wardrobes. whb.
13' 3" x 11' 1"

FRONT BEDROOM 4   Fitted wardrobes.
15' 10" x 11' 3"

BATHROOM   Bath with telephone shower, whb, & wc, part-tiled.

CALZADOS SOLER
BARCELONA

8 Mayo 1994

Sr. D Luis IMedina
Africa, 32
Manresa

Señor:

El próximo día 15 abriré al público un establecimiento dedicado a la venta al por mayor y al detalle de toda clase de zapatos para caballero, señora y niño.

Mi larga experiencia en el negocio calzado me permite asegurar a mi futura clientela que estoy en condiciones de ofrecerle artrículos seleccionados a precios muy ventajosos. Para ello he contratado en firme la producción completa de dos importantes—fábricas mallorquinas que, en el futuro, prepararán sus modelos de acuerdo con mis indicaciones.

Cuando venga a esta, no deje de visitar mi establecimiento pues ola seguridad que los nuevos modelos para verano han de—mar poderosamente su atención.

Actualmente estoy preparando un catálogo de las novedades más—interestantes que voy a presentar al público y tan pronto como me sea posible, tendré sumo placer en remitirle un ejemplar.

Esperando tomará nota de mi oferta y de mi firma y ofreciéndo—me incondicionalmente, reciba atentos saludos de

Luis Soler

LS/ma

2

date

Mr T P Harris

OUTSIDE

REAR GARDEN   South-west facing. Very private.

BOILER HOUSE WITH WC

GARAGE   Fully fitted with shelving.

SIDE PASSAGE

We will be happy to show you around this property. I should point out, however, that we have a number of interested parties who have already made appointments to view and I would advise your urgent attention to this matter. Well-appointed properties in this area are difficult to come by as it is ideally located close to schools, shopping facilities and the new motorway.

If you require any further information please do not hesitate to contact me.

Yours sincerely

name
Residential Division

MEMORANDA

Übung 1

Chef an Sekretärin
Datum: 24.02.94
Betreff: Handtücher in den Waschräumen

Die Mitarbeiter beschweren sich über schmutzige Handtücher in den Waschräumen und Toiletten. Wie können wir Abhilfe schaffen? Bitte stellen Sie fest, welche Möglichkeiten es gibt und welche Kosten entstehen. Termin: 31.03.94

MEMORANDA

von: Elmsmann
an: Martins, Lohmar, Siegbrecht, Alsbach
Datum: 21.04.92
Betreff: Messevorbereitungen, Besprechung am 25. d.M.

Sollten Sie irgendwelche Unterlagan, Dokumente o.ä. haben, die wir zur Besprechung am Donnerstag benötigen, so lassen Sie diese bitte bis Mittwoch meiner Sekretärin, Frau Reiser, zukommen.

MEMORANDA

von: Elmsmann, Personalabteilung
an: alle Mitarbeiter
Datum: 17.03.92
Betreff: Urlaubsregelung

Reichen Sie bitte Ihren Sommerurlaub wenn möglich bis Mitte April bei meiner Sekretärin, Frau Reiser, ein. Die Kollegen mit schulpflichtigen Kindern haben natürlich wie immer Vorrang.
Wer noch Urlaubstage von letzten Kalenderjahr übrig hat, muß diesen bis einschließlich 30.04. nehmen, da der Anspruch sonst verfällt.

Key the following letter on A4 paper in single line spacing.

Attention line

Typed in capitals one clear line space after the date or addressee (see below).

XL INSURANCES

45–50 Shanard Avenue, Dublin 9

Tel 01 324567
Fax 01 324566

5 March 1994

ATTENTION   MR P MURPHY

Down & Co
12 Long Lane
Dublin 8

Dear Sirs

PUBLIC LIABILITY CLAIM

We refer to your letter dated 4 February which has been passed to us for attention. Please note our interest in this matter.

We are presently carrying out investigations into your client's accident. In the interim we would be obliged for a note of the precise acts of negligence and breaches in statutory duty that may be alleged. This information shall be received on a strictly without prejudice basis and solely for investigation purposes.

We would be obliged if you would be prepared to let us have copies of your own medical reports, again on a strictly without prejudice basis and solely for negotiation purposes.

Yours faithfully

Peter Smith

---

5 March 1994

Down & Co
12 Long Lane
Dublin 8

ATTENTION Mr P Murphy

Dear Sirs

COMLETH INTERNATIONAL PLC

Comleth House, North Avenue, Limerick
Tel 01 789 0261   Telex Comleth 7899831

Goethe Universität
Studentisches Reisebüro

Senckenberganlage 2 – 24

6000 Frankfurt/Main

Unsere Zeichen   Kassel
H/Z

03.04.19 - -

Studentenfahrt

Sehr geehrte Damen und Herren,

wir danken Ihnen für Ihren Brief vom 21.03.1980, in dem Sie uns baten, Ihnen für Ihre Studentengruppe vom 16.06. bis 23.06. einschließ lich Zimmer zu reservieren.

Bevor wir uns weiter darum bemühen können, würden wir gerne von Ihnen erfahren, um wieviele Studenten es sich handelt. Ferner möchten wir gerne wissen, in welcher Preisklasse die Zimmer sein sollen. Und welche Mahlzeiten von den jungen Leuten im Hotel eingenommen werden sollen.

Unser Haus würde Ihnen gerne auch Vorschläge unterbreiten bezüglich Ausflugfahrten in die nähere und weitere Umgebung von Kassel.

Wir warten auf Ihre baldige Antwort.

Mit freundlichen Grüßen

Reisebüro Martin

Key the following circular letter and form on separate sheets of A5 paper. Do not leave space for the name and address.

LANSDOWNE SECRETARIAL INSTITUTE
103 Melbourne Road, Bishopstown
Cork
Telephone (021) 79 33 44

Date as postmark

Dear Sir/Madam

This year, as part of our summer programme, we expect to have over 400 students attend our Institute during the months of June, July and August.

We are now contacting those people who kindly agreed to provide accommodation for our students in the past to ascertain whether or not they will be interested in taking further students this year.

The rate this year is £75 per week to include bed, breakfast, packed lunch and evening meal for the seven days. All students will stay for 21 days and will arrive on day flights.

If you feel you can be of assistance to us please complete the enclosed form.

Thanking you for your help.

Yours faithfully

M P HENDERSON
Accommodation Officer

Enc

ACCOMMODATION

NAME ....

ADDRESS ....

TELEPHONE ....

NO OF AVAILABLE ROOMS .... SINGLE .... TWIN ....

WITH/WITHOUT FACILITIES (delete as appropriate)

STUDY FACILITIES? .... YES .... NO...........................

TRANSPORT .... BUS ROUTE(s) .... DART....................

WILL YOU ACCEPT SMOKERS? ....YES .... NO ....

CAN YOU CATER FOR SPECIAL DIETS?

.... VEGETARIAN .... COELIAC .... VEGAN .... DIABETIC

DO YOU HAVE CHILDREN? AGE(s) ....

OTHER COMMENTS ....

....

COMLETH INTERNATIONAL PLC

Comleth House, North Avenue, Limerick
Tel 01 789 0261   Telex Comleth 7899831

Monsieur LUCE
34 avenue de la République
50100 CHERBOURG

Dublin, le 5 mars 1992

N/Réf: TB/ON
V/Réf: JP/LS/67

Objet:

Monsieur,

Nous vous envoyons ce jour un relevé de compte présentant un solde débiteur de 34,50 F sur vos commandes du premier trimestre 19.. Vous voudrez bien vérifier avec votre comptabilité personnelle.

Si vous êtes en accord avec notre document, veuillez envoyer le paiement afin de régulariser la situation. Si toutefois le paiement nous était parvenu entre-temps, nous vous serions obligés de considérer cette lettre comme nulle.

Toujours à vos ordres, nous vous prions de recevoir, Monsieur, nos sincères salutations.

Le service de comptabilité

Thomas BROWN

Marking carbon copies

When finished typing the letter mark it in the following way:

<u>Original</u>
cc Mr K Johnson
   File

<u>1st copy</u>
cc Mr K Johnson ✓
   File

<u>2nd copy</u>
cc Mr K Johnson
   File ✓

Remove letters from machine, tick or underscore one carbon copy for Mr K Johnson and the second copy for File.

Key the following letter on A4 paper. Take two carbon copies and mark one for Mr K Johnson and the other for the file.

XL INSURANCES

45–50 Shanard Avenue, Dublin 9

Tel 01 324567
Fax 01 324566

29 August 1994

Mr H Roberts
Priory House
Edenderry
Co Offaly

Dear Sirs

EMPLOYER'S LIABILITY CLAIM
G H Young V Green & Co

We refer to the above case and to our letter dated 30 July. We have not received a reply from you in connection with the case.

Our further investigations into this matter have superseded the contents of the above letter. We have completed our engineering investigations and obtained our engineering evidence. While in July last it looked as if we had a strong case against this plaintiff, on the basis of present findings, the plaintiff will succeed. There are a number of points for consideration. The basic problem is that the type of cut the plaintiff was making and the positioning of the fence beside the blade guard made it impossible for the guard to operate fully. However, the fencing could and should have been adjusted in order to allow full operation of the guard. It appears that neither the plaintiff nor indeed the supervisory or management staff at Green & Co were aware of this adjustment. Furthermore, there is an accessory, known as a clamping device, for this machine which if used would have avoided the necessity for the plaintiff placing his fingers near the blade. This clamping device was not purchased with the machine.

We confirm that we will shortly open negotiations with the plaintiff and will dispose of this case on the best terms available. We shall advise you of the outcome of negotiations when completed.

In the meantime, please note there is an excess of IR£2,500 under the policy. Perhaps you would obtain monies from your client in this regard and forward same to us.

Yours faithfully

B A Fitzpatrick

COMLETH INTERNATIONAL PLC

Comleth House, North Avenue, Limerick
Tel 01 789 0261   Telex Comleth 7899831

Monsieur FREAN
19 rue Jussieu
75005 PARIS

Dublin, le 5 mars 1994

V/Réf: MP/735
N/Réf: AR/RB

Objet:

Monsieur,

Nous vous remercions de l'attention que vous portez à nos fabrications.

Nos ateliers de taille de pierre, terre cuite, marbrerie, notre magasin d'exposition (25 cheminées présentées) ouverts tous les jours de 8h à 12h30 et de, 13h30 à 19h, sont prêts à vous accueillir. Notre bureau d'études étudiera tous les problèmes particuliers concernant votre cheminée à feu de bois, votre salle de bains en marbre, vos dallages, escaliers, etc...

Dans l'attente de votre visite, nous vous prions de recevoir, Monsieur, nos sincères salutations.

Le Directeur

Michel ARNAUD

This is a short business letter typed in single spacing on an A5 letterhead. (Design your own letterhead.) Leave at least 1" clear after the letterhead before the beginning of the letter.

DERMOT O'NEILL

Dental Surgeon
4 Fitzwilliam Place, Dublin 2

Telephone 6791213 Fax 6791214

16 February 1993

Ms Dolores O'Keeffe
23 The Rise
Mount Merrion
CO DUBLIN

Dear Ms O'Keeffe

Your next check-up will take place on Friday 23 February at 11.30 am. Please contact me, by return, if this time is not convenient for you.

Yours sincerely

OLWYN STEPHENS
Receptionist

Key the following business letter using the letterhead provided. Supply an appropriate name, address and date.

Dear

Thank you for your application and enclosed curriculum vitae.

Unfortunately, we do not have any vacancies at the moment suitable to your qualifications and experience. However, we will be pleased to hold your details on file and will contact you should a vacancy arise.

Thanking you for the interest you have shown in XL Enterprises. We wish you every success in the future.

Yours sincerely

Personnel Officer

Foreign language letters

The following examples show the layout/display used in Irish, French, German and Spanish letters. Accents can be inserted with a black pen or you may have the facility of using a language golfball or daisywheel. If using a computer you may also be able to switch your keyboard to a foreign language mode.

Personal letters

Since you will not be using headed paper it will be necessary to insert <u>your</u> address. The following gives you a choice of places where this may be inserted:

a) Centered across page
b) Flush with right margin
c) Left margin, one clear line above date

Key the following personal letters on A5 paper in single line spacing.

"Minerva"
Ashford
Co Wicklow

20 September 1994

The Secretary
Ocean Sailing club
Dun Laoghaire
Co Dublin

Dear Sir/Madam

Please forward an application form for membership of your club.

I have just returned from Australia where I developed a keen interest in sailing. The Ocean Sailing Club has been recommended to me by several colleagues and I would welcome the opportunity of becoming a member.

Yours faithfully

MILES OAKLEY

23 The Rise
Mount Merrion
CO DUBLIN
24 February 1993

Mr Dermot O'Neill
Dental Surgeon
4 Fitzwilliam Place
DUBLIN 2

Dear Mr O'Neill

This letter will confirm my telephone conversation with your receptionist, Olwyn, this morning.

Regrettably, I will be unable to attend for my six-monthly check-up on Tuesday next as I am scheduled to sit my driving test on that day.

I apologise if this late cancellation causes any inconvenience and I will telephone Olwyn at the beginning of next week to re-schedule the appointment.

Yours sincerely

DOLORES O'KEEFFE

Envelopes

o   Make sure the envelope is large enough for the letter and possible enclosure.

o   Type the first line of the name and address approximately half way down and one-third across.

o   When typing an Irish address, type the county in capitals or underscore.

o   When typing an English address, type the postal town in capitals and postal code on a separate line.

o   Type in single line spacing using open punctuation.

o   PERSONAL, URGENT, CONFIDENTIAL: type in capitals two line spaces above the name and address.

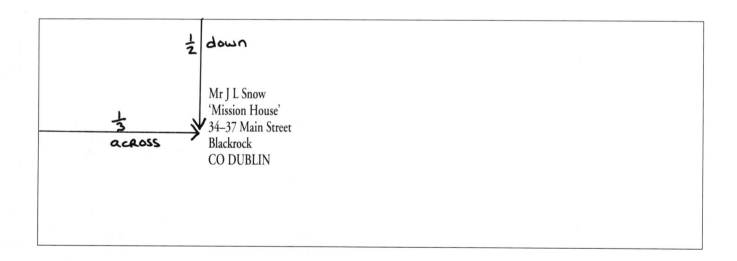

XL INSURANCES

45-50 Shanard Avenue, Dublin 9

Tel 01 324567
Fax 01 324566

XL INSURANCES

45-50 Shanard Avenue, Dublin 9

Tel 01 324567
Fax 01 324566

XL INSURANCES

45-50 Shanard Avenue, Dublin 9

Tel 01 324567
Fax 01 324566

XL INSURANCES

45-50 Shanard Avenue, Dublin 9

Tel 01 324567
Fax 01 324566

XL INSURANCES

45-50 Shanard Avenue, Dublin 9

Tel 01 324567
Fax 01 324566

XL INSURANCES

45-50 Shanard Avenue, Dublin 9

Tel 01 324567
Fax 01 324566